Spanish Cook

Traditional Spanish Cuisine, Delicious Recipes from Spain that Anyone Can Cook at Home

Louise Wynn

Copyright © 2020 by Louise Wynn

All rights reserved. No part of this book may be reproduced or used in any manner without written permission of the copyright owner except for the use of quotations in a book review and certain other non-commercial uses permitted by copyright law.

Table of Contents

Pinchitos moruños 6
Marinated mushrooms 8
La calçotada 10
Pan-fried ham and vegetables with eggs 12
Chargrilled squid 14
Mojete 16
Crumbed chicken with green mayonnaise 18
Patatas bravas 21
Chilled almond soup with grapes 23
Fish soup with orange 25
Spinach empanadillas 27
Broad beans with bacon 29
Seafood paella 31
Hake and clams with salsa verde 33
Mussels with a parsley crust 35
Potato tortilla 37
Calderete of rice with fish and aioli 39
Marmitako 42
Vieiras de Santiago 44
Spinach with raisins and pine nuts 46
Zarzuela 48
Braised cabbage with chorizo 51
Escalivada 52
Chilled avocado soup with cumin 54
Ensaladilla 56
Spicy sausage and cheese tortilla 58
Calamares rellenos 60
Pisto manchego 62
Scrambled eggs with spring asparagus 64
Olive and anchovy bites 66
Gazpacho 68
Mushroom, bean and chorizo salad 70

Spiced clams	72
Flash-fried squid with paprika and garlic	74
Buñuelos	76
Chicharrones	78
Flamenco eggs	79
Rice tortitas	81
Sizzling prawns	83
King prawns in crispy batter	84
Tapas of almonds, olives and cheese	86
Artichoke rice cakes with Manchego	91
Stewed aubergine	93
Sopa de mariscos	95
Tortilla with beans	97
Chicken with lemon and garlic	99
Avocado, orange and almond salad	101
Scrambled eggs with prawns	103
Charred artichokes with lemon oil dip	104
San Esteban canelones	106
Paella Valenciana	108
Simple rice salad	111
Pimiento tartlets	113
Andrajos	115
Orange chicken salad	117
Cuban-style rice	119
Sopa Castiliana	121
Catalan broad bean and potato soup	123
Barbecued mini ribs	125
Vegetable rice pot	127
Butterflied prawns in chocolate sauce	129
Stuffed tomatoes and peppers	131
Sherried onion soup with saffron	133
Menestra	135
Lentils with mushrooms and anis	137

Chicken croquettes 139
Amanida 141
Moors and Christians 143

Pinchitos moruños

SERVES 4

2.5ml/1/2 tsp cumin seeds

2.5ml/1/2 tsp coriander seeds

2 garlic cloves, finely chopped

5ml/1 tsp paprika

2.5ml/1/2 tsp dried oregano

15ml/1 tbsp lemon juice

45ml/3 tbsp olive oil

500g/11/4lb lean cubed pork

salt and ground black pepper

Instructions

Starting a couple of hours in advance, grind the cumin and coriander seeds in a mortar and work in the garlic with a pinch of salt. Add the paprika and oregano and mix in the lemon juice. Stir in the oil.

Cut the pork into small cubes, then skewer them, three or four at a time, on to cocktail sticks (toothpicks). Put the skewered meat in a shallow dish, and pour over the marinade. Spoon the marinade back over the meat to ensure that it is well coated. Leave to marinate in a cool place for 2 hours.

Preheat the grill (broiler) to high, and line the grill pan with foil. Spread the kebabs out in a row and place under the grill, close to the heat. Cook for about 3 minutes on each side, spooning the juices over when you turn them, until cooked through. Sprinkle with salt and pepper, and serve.

Nutritional information per portion: Energy 233kcal/970kJ; Protein 27g; Carbohydrate 0.7g, of which sugars 0g; Fat 13.5g, of which saturates 2.9g; Cholesterol 79mg; Calcium 25mg; Fibre 0.6g; Sodium 99mg.

Marinated mushrooms

SERVES 4

30ml/2 tbsp olive oil

1 small onion, very finely chopped

1 garlic clove, finely chopped

15ml/1 tbsp tomato purée (paste)

50ml/2fl oz/1/4 cup amontillado sherry

50ml/2fl oz/1/4 cup water

2 cloves

225g/8oz/3 cups button (white) mushrooms, trimmed salt and ground black pepper chopped fresh parsley, to garnish

Instructions

Heat the oil in a pan. Add the onion and garlic and cook until soft. Stir in the tomato purée, sherry, water and cloves, and season to taste. Bring to the boil, cover and simmer gently for 45 minutes. Add more water if it becomes too dry.

Add the mushrooms to the pan, then cover and simmer for about 5 minutes. Remove from the heat and allow to cool, still covered. Chill in the refrigerator overnight. Serve the mushrooms cold, sprinkled with the chopped fresh parsley.

Nutritional information per portion: Energy 80kcal/329kJ; Protein 1.4g; Carbohydrate 2.1g, of which sugars 1.7g; Fat 5.8g, of which saturates 0.9g; Cholesterol 0mg; Calcium 9mg; Fibre 0.9g; Sodium 14mg.

La calçotada

SERVES 6

3 bunches of plump spring onions (scallions), or Chinese green onions, which are about 2.5cm/1in across the bulb

olive oil, for brushing

FOR THE ROMESCO SAUCE

2–3 ñoras or other mild dried red chillies, such as Mexican anchos or guajillos

1 large red (bell) pepper, halved and seeded

2 large tomatoes, halved and seeded

4–6 large garlic cloves, unpeeled

75–90ml/5–6 tbsp olive oil

25g/1oz/1/4 cup hazelnuts, blanched

4 slices French bread, each about 2cm/3/4in thick

15ml/1 tbsp sherry vinegar squeeze of lemon juice (optional)

Instructions

Soak the dried chillies in hot water for about 30 minutes. Preheat the oven to 220°C/425°F/Gas 7. Place the pepper, tomatoes and garlic on a baking sheet and drizzle with 15ml/1 tbsp olive oil. Roast, uncovered, for 30–40 minutes, until the pepper is blistered and blackened and the garlic is soft. Cool slightly, then peel the pepper, tomatoes and garlic.

Heat the remaining oil in a small frying pan and fry the hazelnuts until lightly browned, then transfer them to a plate. Fry the bread in the same oil until light brown on both sides, then transfer to the plate with the nuts and leave to cool. Reserve the oil from cooking.

Drain the chillies, discard as many of their seeds as you can, then place the chillies in a food processor. Add the red pepper halves, tomatoes, garlic, hazelnuts and bread chunks together with the reserved olive oil. Add the vinegar and process to a paste. Check the seasoning and thin the sauce with a little more oil or lemon juice, if necessary. Set aside.

Trim the roots from the spring onions or trim the Chinese onion leaves so that they are about 15–18cm/6–7in long. Brush with oil. Heat an oiled ridged griddle and cook the onions for about 2 minutes on each side, turning once and brushing with oil. Serve at once with the sauce.

Nutritional information per portion: Energy 214kcal/896kJ; Protein 5.2g; Carbohydrate 21g, of which sugars 5.3g; Fat 12.8g, of which saturates 1.7g; Cholesterol 0mg; Calcium 64mg; Fibre 2.8g; Sodium 173mg.

Pan-fried ham and vegetables with eggs

SERVES 4

30ml/2 tbsp olive oil

1 onion, roughly chopped

2 garlic cloves, finely chopped

175g/6oz cooked ham

225g/8oz courgettes (zucchini)

1 red (bell) pepper, seeded and thinly sliced

1 yellow (bell) pepper, seeded and thinly sliced 10ml/2 tsp paprika

400g/14oz can chopped tomatoes

15ml/1 tbsp sun-dried tomato paste

4 large (US extra large) eggs

115g/4oz/1 cup coarsely grated Cheddar cheese salt and ground black pepper crusty bread, to serve

Ingredients

Heat the olive oil in a deep frying pan. Add the onion and garlic and cook for 4 minutes, stirring frequently.

Meanwhile, cut the cooked ham and courgettes into 5cm/2in batons.

Add the courgettes and peppers to the pan and cook over a medium heat for 3–4 minutes.

Stir in the paprika, tomatoes, tomato paste, ham and seasoning. Bring to a simmer and cook over a gentle heat for 15 minutes.

Reduce the heat to low. Make four wells in the tomato mixture, break an egg into each and season. Cook over a gentle heat until the white begins to set.

Preheat the grill (broiler). Sprinkle the cheese over and grill (broil) for about 5 minutes until the eggs are set. Serve with crusty bread.

Nutritional information per portion: Energy 357kcal/1487kJ; Protein 24.8g; Carbohydrate 12.2g, of which sugars 10.7g; Fat 23.1g, of which saturates 9.4g; Cholesterol 244mg; Calcium 280mg; Fibre 3.1g; Sodium 817mg.

Chargrilled squid

SERVES 4

2 whole cleaned squid, with tentacles, about 275g/10oz each

75ml/5 tbsp olive oil

30ml/2 tbsp sherry vinegar

2 fresh red chillies, finely chopped

60ml/4 tbsp dry white wine

salt and ground black pepper

hot cooked rice, to serve

15–30ml/1–2 tbsp chopped parsley, to garnish

Instructions

Make a cut down the side of the body of each squid, then open it out flat. Score the flesh on both sides of the bodies in a criss-cross pattern. Chop the tentacles into short lengths. Place all the pieces in a non-metallic dish.

Whisk together the oil and vinegar in a bowl. Add salt and pepper to taste, pour over the squid and toss to mix. Cover and leave to marinate for 1 hour.

Heat a ridged griddle pan until hot. Add the body of one of the squid and cook over a medium heat for 2–3 minutes, pressing the squid with a metal spatula to make sure it stays flat. Repeat on the other side. Cook the other squid body in the same way.

Cut the squid bodies into diagonal strips and arrange on the rice. Keep hot. Add the tentacles and chillies to the pan and toss over a medium heat for 2 minutes. Stir in the wine, then drizzle over the squid. Garnish with parsley.

Nutritional information per portion: Energy 258kcal/1076kJ; Protein 23.5g; Carbohydrate 2g, of which sugars 0.2g; Fat 16.4g, of which saturates 2.6g; Cholesterol 338mg; Calcium 25mg; Fibre 0g; Sodium 167mg.

Mojete

SERVES 8

2 red (bell) peppers

2 yellow (bell) peppers

1 red onion, sliced

2 garlic cloves, halved

50g/2oz/1/4 cup black olives

6 large ripe tomatoes, quartered

5ml/1 tsp soft light brown sugar

45ml/3 tbsp amontillado sherry

3–4 fresh rosemary sprigs

30ml/2 tbsp olive oil

salt and ground black pepper

fresh bread, to serve

Instructions

Halve the peppers and remove the seeds. Cut each pepper lengthways into 12 strips. Preheat the oven to 200°C/400°F/Gas 6.

Place the peppers, onion, garlic, olives and tomatoes in a large roasting pan.

Sprinkle the vegetables with the sugar, then pour in the sherry. Season well with salt and pepper, cover with foil and bake for 45 minutes.

4 Remove the foil from the pan and stir the mixture well. Add the rosemary sprigs and drizzle with the olive oil. Return the pan to the oven and cook for a further 30 minutes, uncovered, until the vegetables are very tender. Serve hot or cold with chunks of fresh crusty bread.

Nutritional information per portion: Energy 75kcal/313kJ; Protein 1.3g; Carbohydrate 7.5g, of which sugars 7.2g; Fat 3.9g, of which saturates 0.6g; Cholesterol 0mg; Calcium 17mg; Fibre 2g; Sodium 151mg.

Crumbed chicken with green mayonnaise

SERVES 4

4 chicken breast fillets, each weighing about 200g/7oz

juice of 1 lemon

5ml/1 tsp paprika

plain (all-purpose) flour, for dusting

1–2 eggs

dried breadcrumbs, for coating

about 60ml/4 tbsp olive oil

salt and ground black pepper

lemon wedges, to serve (optional)

FOR THE MAYONNAISE

120ml/4fl oz/1/2 cup mayonnaise

30ml/2 tbsp pickled capers, drained and chopped 30ml/2 tbsp chopped fresh parsley

Instructions

Start a couple of hours ahead, if you can. Skin the chicken fillets. Lay them outside down and, with a sharp knife, cut horizontally, almost through, from the rounded side. Open them up like a book. Press gently, to make a roundish shape, the size of a side plate. Sprinkle with lemon juice and paprika.

Set out three plates. Sprinkle flour over one, seasoning it well. Beat the egg with a little salt and pour into the second. Sprinkle the third with dried breadcrumbs. Dip the fillets first into the flour on both sides, then into the egg, then into the breadcrumbs. Chill the crumbed chicken, if you have time.

Put the mayonnaise ingredients in a bowl and mix well to combine.

Heat the oil in a heavy frying pan over a high heat. Fry the fillets, two at a time, turning after 3 minutes, until golden on both sides. Add more oil for the second batch if needed. Serve at once, with the mayonnaise and lemon wedges, if using.

Nutritional information per portion: Energy 594kcal/2476kJ; Protein 52g; Carbohydrate 12.5g, of which sugars 1.1g; Fat 37.7g, of which saturates 6g; Cholesterol 210mg; Calcium 64mg; Fibre 1g; Sodium 372mg.

Sweet and salty vegetable crisps

SERVES 4

1 small fresh beetroot (beet)

caster (superfine) sugar and fine salt, for sprinkling

olive oil, for frying

coarse sea salt, to serve

Instructions

Peel the beetroot and, using a mandolin or a vegetable peeler, cut it into very thin slices.

Lay the slices on kitchen paper and sprinkle them with sugar and fine salt.

Heat 5cm/2in oil in a deep pan until a cube of bread turns golden in 1 minute. Cook the slices in batches, until they float to the surface and turn golden at the edge. Drain on kitchen paper and sprinkle with sea salt once they are cool.

Nutritional information per portion: Energy 155kcal/639kJ; Protein 0.3g; Carbohydrate 1.4g, of which sugars 1.3g; Fat 6.5g, of which saturates 2.4g; Cholesterol 0mg; Calcium 4mg; Fibre 0.4g; Sodium 13mg.

Patatas bravas

SERVES 4

675g/1 1/2lb small new potatoes

75ml/5 tbsp olive oil

2 garlic cloves, sliced

3 dried chillies, seeded and chopped

2.5ml/1/2 tsp ground cumin

10ml/2 tsp paprika

30ml/2 tbsp red or white wine vinegar

1 red or green (bell) pepper, seeded and sliced coarse sea salt, for sprinkling (optional)

Instructions

Scrub the potatoes and put them into a pan of salted water. Bring to the boil and cook for 10 minutes, or until almost tender. Drain and leave to cool slightly.

Peel, if you like, then cut into chunks. Heat the oil in a frying or sauté pan and fry the potatoes, turning them frequently, until golden.

Meanwhile, crush together the garlic cloves, the chillies and cumin using a mortar and pestle. Mix the paste with the paprika and wine vinegar, then add to the potatoes with the pepper and cook, stirring, for 2 minutes. Sprinkle with salt, if using, and serve hot as a tapas dish or cold as a side dish.

Nutritional information per portion: Energy 256kcal/1070kJ; Protein 3.3g; Carbohydrate 30g, of which sugars 4.9g; Fat 14.4g, of which saturates 2.2g; Cholesterol 0mg; Calcium 14mg; Fibre 2.4g; Sodium 20mg.

Chilled almond soup with grapes

SERVES 6

115g/4oz stale white bread

115g/4oz/1 cup blanched almonds

2 garlic cloves, sliced

75ml/5 tbsp olive oil

25ml/1 1/2 tbsp sherry vinegar

salt and ground black pepper

FOR THE GARNISH

toasted flaked (sliced) almonds

green and black grapes, halved and seeded chopped fresh chives

Instructions

Break the bread into a bowl and pour in 150ml/1/4 pint/2/3 cup cold water. Leave to soak for about 5 minutes, then squeeze dry.

Put the almonds and garlic in a food processor or blender and process until very finely ground. Add the soaked white bread and process again until thoroughly combined.

Continue to process, gradually adding the oil until the mixture forms a smooth paste. Add the sherry vinegar, followed by 600ml/1 pint/2 1/2 cups cold water and process until the mixture is smooth.

Transfer the soup to a bowl and season with plenty of salt and pepper, adding a little more water if the soup is very thick. Cover with clear film (plastic wrap) and chill for at least 2 hours.

Ladle the soup into bowls. Sprinkle the almonds, halved grapes and chopped chives over to garnish.

Nutritional information per portion: Energy 246kcal/1023kJ; Protein 5.8g; Carbohydrate 11.1g, of which sugars 1.3g; Fat 20.2g, of which saturates 2.2g; Cholesterol 0mg; Calcium 67mg; Fibre 1.8g; Sodium 103mg.

Fish soup with orange

SERVES 6

1kg/2 1/4lb small hake or whiting, whole but cleaned

1.2 litres/2 pints/5 cups water

4 bitter oranges or 4 sweet oranges and 2 lemons

30ml/2 tbsp olive oil

5 garlic cloves, unpeeled

1 large onion, finely chopped

1 tomato, peeled, seeded and chopped

4 small potatoes, cut into rounds

5ml/1 tsp paprika

salt and ground black pepper

15–30ml/1–2 tbsp finely chopped fresh parsley, to garnish

Instructions

Fillet the fish and cut each fillet into three, reserving all the trimmings. Put the fillets on a plate, salt lightly and chill. Put the trimmings in a pan, add the water and a spiral of orange rind. Bring to a simmer, skim, then cover and cook gently for 30 minutes.

Heat the oil in a large pan over a high heat. Smash the garlic cloves with the flat of a knife and fry until they are well coloured. Discard them and turn down the heat. Fry the onion gently until it is softened, adding the tomato halfway through.

Strain in the hot fish stock (adding the orange spiral as well if you wish) and bring back to the boil. Add the potatoes to the pan and cook them for about 5 minutes.

Add the fish pieces to the soup, a few at a time, without letting it go off the boil. Cook for about 15 minutes. Add the squeezed orange juice and lemon juice, if using, and the paprika, with salt and pepper to taste. Serve in bowls, garnished with a little parsley.

Nutritional information per portion: Energy 223kcal/937kJ; Protein 18.3g; Carbohydrate 25.2g, of which sugars 11.7g; Fat 6.1g, of which saturates 0.9g; Cholesterol 19mg; Calcium 86mg; Fibre 3.5g; Sodium 103mg.

Spinach empanadillas

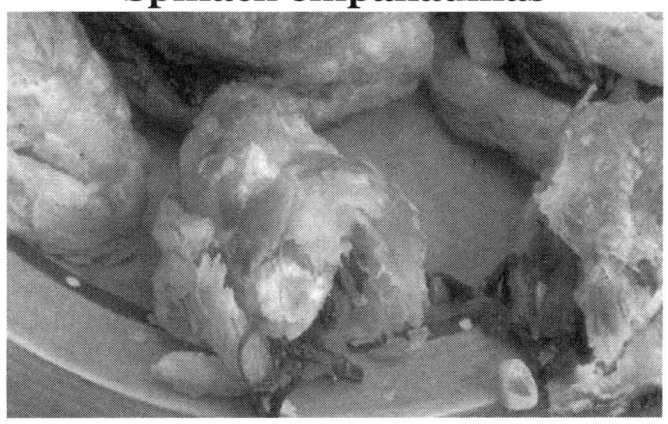

MAKES 20

25g/1oz/1/4 cup raisins

25ml/1 1/2 tbsp olive oil

450g/1lb fresh spinach leaves, washed, drained and chopped

6 canned anchovies, drained and chopped

2 garlic cloves, finely chopped

25g/1oz/1/4 cup pine nuts, roughly chopped

350g/12oz puff pastry

1 egg, beaten

salt and ground black pepper

Instructions

To make the filling, soak the raisins in warm water for 10 minutes. Drain well, then chop them roughly.

Heat the olive oil in a pan, add the spinach, stir, then cover and cook over a low heat for about 2 minutes until the spinach starts to wilt. Remove the lid, turn up the heat and cook until any liquid has evaporated.

Add the anchovies, garlic and seasoning to the spinach and cook, stirring, for 1 minute. Remove from the heat. Stir in the raisins and pine nuts. Cool.

Meanwhile, preheat the oven to 180ºC/350ºF/Gas 4. Roll out the pastry on a lightly floured surface to a 3mm/1/8in thickness.

Using a 7.5cm/3in pastry cutter, cut the pastry into 20 rounds. Place about 10ml/2 tsp filling in the middle of each round, then brush the edges with a little water. Bring up the sides of the pastry and seal well. Press the edges together with the back of a fork. Brush with egg.

Place the pies on a greased baking sheet and bake for 15 minutes, or until puffed up and golden. Transfer the pies to a wire rack to cool. Serve warm.

Nutritional information per empanadilla: Energy 100kcal/416kJ; Protein 2.4g; Carbohydrate 8.1g, of which sugars 1.8g; Fat 6.8g, of which saturates 0.3g; Cholesterol 10mg; Calcium 62mg; Fibre 0.8g; Sodium 98mg.

Broad beans with bacon

SERVES 4

30ml/2 tbsp olive oil

1 small onion, finely chopped

1 garlic clove, finely chopped

50g/2oz rindless smoked streaky (fatty) bacon, roughly chopped

225g/8oz broad (fava) beans, thawed if frozen

5ml/1 tsp paprika

15ml/1 tbsp sweet sherry

salt and ground black pepper

Instructions

Heat the olive oil in a large frying pan or sauté pan. Add the chopped onion, garlic and bacon and fry over a high heat for about 5 minutes, stirring frequently, until the onion is softened and the bacon browned.

Add the beans and paprika to the pan and stir-fry for 1 minute. Add the sherry, lower the heat, cover and cook for 5–10 minutes until the beans are tender. Season with salt and pepper and serve hot or warm.

Nutritional information per portion: Energy 139kcal/577kJ; Protein 6.8g; Carbohydrate 8.2g, of which sugars 1.6g; Fat 9g, of which saturates 1.9g; Cholesterol 8mg; Calcium 38mg; Fibre 3.9g; Sodium 163mg.

Seafood paella

SERVES 4

45ml/3 tbsp olive oil

1 Spanish onion, chopped

2 large garlic cloves, chopped

150g/5oz frying chorizo, sliced

300g/11oz small squid, cleaned

1 red (bell) pepper, cut into strips

4 tomatoes, peeled, seeded and diced, or 200g/7oz can tomatoes

500ml/17fl oz/2 1/4 cups chicken stock, plus a little extra

105ml/7 tbsp dry white wine

200g/7oz/1 cup paella rice

pinch of saffron threads (0.2g), crumbled

150g/5oz/generous 1 cup peas

12 large cooked prawns (shrimp), in the shell, or 8 peeled scampi (extra large shrimp)

450g/1lb fresh mussels, scrubbed

450g/1lb clams, scrubbed

4 cooked king prawns (jumbo shrimp) or scampi, in the shell salt and ground black pepper

chopped fresh parsley and lemon wedges, to garnish

Instructions

Heat the olive oil in a paella pan or large frying pan, add the onion and garlic and fry until translucent. Add the chorizo and fry until lightly golden.

Cut the bodies of the squids into rings and the tentacles into pieces. Add the squid to the pan and sauté over a high heat for 2 minutes.

Stir in the pepper and tomatoes and simmer gently for 5 minutes, until the pepper is tender. Pour in the stock and wine, stir well and bring to the boil. Stir in the rice and saffron and season well. Bring the liquid back to the boil, then lower the heat and simmer for about 10 minutes.

Gently stir the peas, prawns or scampi, mussels and clams into the rice, then cook for a further 15–20 minutes, until the rice is tender and all the mussels and clams have opened. (Discard any that remain closed.)

Remove the pan from the heat and arrange the king prawns or scampi on top. Cover and leave to stand for 5 minutes. Sprinkle the paella with chopped parsley and serve from the pan, accompanied by lemon wedges.

Nutritional information per portion: Energy 585kcal/2445kJ; Protein 36.1g; Carbohydrate 60.9g, of which sugars 10.1g; Fat 20.4g, of which saturates 5.6g; Cholesterol 268mg; Calcium 132mg; Fibre 4.2g; Sodium 1055mg.

Hake and clams with salsa verde

SERVES 4

4 hake steaks, about 2cm/3/4in thick

50g/2oz/1/2 cup plain (all-purpose) flour, for dusting, plus 30ml/2 tbsp

60ml/4 tbsp olive oil

15ml/1 tbsp lemon juice

1 small onion, finely chopped

4 garlic cloves, finely chopped

150ml/1/4 pint/2/3 cup fish stock

150ml/1/4 pint/2/3 cup white wine

90ml/6 tbsp chopped fresh parsley

75g/3oz/3/4 cup frozen petits pois

16 fresh clams, cleaned

salt and ground black pepper

Instructions

Preheat the oven to 180°C/350°F/Gas 4. Season the fish, then dust with flour.

Heat half the oil in a large pan, add the fish and fry for 1 minute on each side.

Transfer to an ovenproof dish and sprinkle with the lemon juice.

Heat the remaining oil in a clean pan and fry the onion and garlic, stirring, until soft. Stir in the 30ml/2 tbsp flour and cook for about 1 minute.

Slowly add the stock and wine to the pan, stirring until thickened. Add 75ml/5 tbsp of the parsley and the petits pois to the sauce and season with plenty of salt and pepper.

Pour the sauce over the fish, and bake for 15–20 minutes, adding the clams 3–4 minutes before the end of the cooking time.

Discard any clams that do not open once cooked, then sprinkle the fish with the remaining parsley and serve.

Nutritional information per portion: Energy 347kcal/1449kJ; Protein 34.2g; Carbohydrate 13.2g, of which sugars 1.4g; Fat 15.2g, of which saturates 2.2g; Cholesterol 51mg; Calcium 109mg; Fibre 2.4g; Sodium 460mg.

Mussels with a parsley crust

SERVES 4

450g/1lb fresh mussels

45ml/3 tbsp water

15ml/1 tbsp melted butter

15ml/1 tbsp olive oil

45ml/3 tbsp freshly grated Parmesan cheese

30ml/2 tbsp chopped fresh parsley

2 garlic cloves, finely chopped

2.5ml/1/2 tsp coarsely ground black pepper crusty bread, to serve

Instructions

Scrub the mussels thoroughly, scraping off any barnacles with a round-bladed knife and pulling out the gritty beards. Sharply tap any open mussels and discard any that fail to close or whose shells are broken.

Place the mussels in a large pan and add the water. Cover the pan with a lid and steam for about 5 minutes, or until the mussel shells have opened.

Drain the mussels well and discard any that remain closed. Carefully snap off the top shell from each mussel, leaving the actual flesh still attached to the bottom shell.

Balance the shells upright in a flameproof dish, packing them closely together to make sure that they stay level.

Preheat the grill (broiler) to high. Put the melted butter, olive oil, Parmesan cheese, parsley, garlic and black pepper in a small bowl and mix well to combine.

Spoon a small amount of the cheese and garlic mixture on top of each mussel and gently press down with the back of the spoon.

Grill (broil) the mussels for about 2 minutes, or until they are sizzling and golden. Serve the mussels in their shells, with bread to mop up the juices.

Nutritional information per portion: Energy 110kcal/456kJ; Protein 5.4g; Carbohydrate 0.3g, of which sugars 0.3g; Fat 9.7g, of which saturates 4.7g; Cholesterol 21mg; Calcium 165mg; Fibre 0.6g; Sodium 156mg.

Potato tortilla

SERVES 6

450g/1lb small waxy potatoes, peeled

1 Spanish onion

45ml/3 tbsp vegetable oil

4 large (US extra large) eggs

salt and ground black pepper

fresh flat leaf parsley or tomato wedges, to garnish

Instructions

Using a sharp knife, cut the potatoes into thin slices and slice the onion into thin rings. Heat 30ml/2 tbsp of the oil in a 20cm/8in heavy frying pan.

Add the potatoes and the onions to the pan and cook over a low heat for 20 minutes, or until the potato slices are just tender. Remove from the heat.

In a large bowl, beat together the eggs with a little salt and pepper. Stir in the potatoes and onion.

Clean the frying pan with kitchen paper then heat the remaining oil and pour in the potato mixture. Cook very gently for 5–8 minutes until set underneath. During cooking, lift the edges of the tortilla with a spatula, and allow any uncooked egg to run underneath. Shake the pan from side to side, to prevent sticking.

Place a large heatproof plate upside-down over the pan, invert the tortilla on to the plate and then slide it back into the pan. Cook for 2–3 minutes more, until the underside of the tortilla is golden brown. Cut into wedges and serve, garnished with fresh flat leaf parsley or tomato wedges.

Nutritional information per portion: Energy 163kcal/681kJ; Protein 5.8g; Carbohydrate 14.7g, of which sugars 2.8g; Fat 9.5g, of which saturates 1.9g; Cholesterol 127mg; Calcium 32mg; Fibre 1.2g; Sodium 56mg.

Calderete of rice with fish and aioli

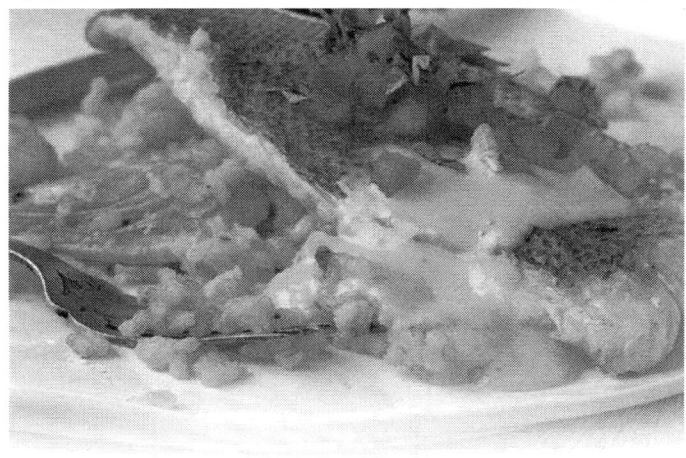

SERVES 6

1.6kg/3 1/2lb mixed fish on the bone, such as snapper, bream, grey or red mullet, or bass

45ml/3 tbsp olive oil

6 garlic cloves, smashed

1 ñora chilli or 1 hot dried chilli, seeded and chopped

250g/9oz ripe tomatoes, peeled, seeded and chopped pinch of saffron threads (0.25g)

30ml/2 tbsp dry vermouth or white wine

1 tomato, finely diced

30ml/2 tbsp chopped fresh parsley

400g/14oz/2 cups paella rice, washed

115g/4oz small unshelled shrimps

salt and ground black pepper

FOR THE STOCK

1 onion, chopped

2 garlic cloves, chopped

1 celery stick, chopped

1 carrot, chopped

1 litre/1 3/4 pints/4 cups water

FOR THE AIOLI

4 garlic cloves, finely chopped

2.5ml/1/2 tsp salt

5ml/1 tsp lemon juice

2 egg yolks

250ml/8fl oz/1 cup olive oil

Instructions

Remove the heads from the fish. Working from the head end, cut the skin along the top of the back and work the fillets off the bone. Trim as needed, put the fillets on a plate and salt them lightly. Cover and place in the refrigerator until required.

Make the fish stock. Put the bones, heads, tails and any other remaining bits into a large pan with the onion, garlic, celery, carrot and water. Bring to the boil, then reduce the heat, cover and simmer for about 30 minutes.

Make the aioli. Put the garlic in a large mortar with the salt and lemon juice and reduce to a purée. Add the egg yolks and mix thoroughly. Gradually work in the oil, drop by drop at first, to make a thick, mayonnaise-like sauce.

Put 15ml/1 tbsp of the olive oil in a small pan and add the whole smashed garlic cloves and dried chilli pieces. Fry for a few minutes until the garlic looks roasted.

Add the chopped tomatoes halfway through, crumble in the saffron and cook to form a sauce. Pour the sauce into a small blender and purée until smooth.

Heat the remaining 30ml/2 tbsp oil in a large frying pan and fry the fish pieces until they begin to stiffen. Strain the fish stock into a jug (pitcher), then add 900ml/1 1/2 pints/3 3/4 cups stock and the tomato sauce to the fish. Cook the fish gently for a further 3–4 minutes, until slightly underdone.

Remove the fish pieces from the pan with a slotted spoon to a serving dish. Season lightly and sprinkle with the vermouth or wine, diced tomato and parsley. Cover with foil and keep warm.

Add the rice to the stock, stir, season and bring to a simmer. Cook for 18–20 minutes. Before all the liquid is absorbed, stir in the shrimps. When the rice is tender, cover and turn off the heat. Stand until all the liquid is absorbed: about 5 minutes. Serve from the pan, accompanied by the aioli. When the rice course is almost finished, uncover the fish. Stir the fish juices into the remains of the aioli, then pour over the fish. Eat on the same plates as the rice.

Nutritional information per portion: Energy 720kcal/2996kJ; Protein 31.3g; Carbohydrate 55g, of which sugars 1.8g; Fat 40.8g, of which saturates 5.6g; Cholesterol 136mg; Calcium 133mg; Fibre 0.6g; Sodium 873mg.

Marmitako

SERVES 4

60ml/4 tbsp olive oil

1 onion, chopped

2 garlic cloves, finely chopped

3 green (bell) peppers, seeded and chopped

1/2 dried hot chilli, seeded and chopped

4 light tuna or bonito steaks, about 150g/5oz each

400g/14oz can tomatoes with juice 10ml/2 tsp paprika

3 potatoes, diced

350ml/12fl oz/1 1/2 cups dry (hard) cider salt and ground black pepper

30ml/2 tbsp chopped fresh parsley, to garnish

Instructions

Heat half the oil in a heavy pan big enough to take the fish. Fry the onion gently until softened, then add the garlic. Add the chopped peppers and chilli and stir-fry gently.

Season the fish steaks. Heat the remaining oil in a frying pan and fry the fish steaks for 2 minutes on each side over a high heat. Add the tomatoes to the vegetables and stir-fry briefly. Add the paprika, then season with salt and pepper to taste.

Slip the fish steaks into the sauce, moving the peppers into the spaces between them. Cover with the potatoes, pushing them as flat as possible. Add the cider and bring to a simmer. Cover and cook very gently for about 45 minutes, or until the potatoes are done. Check the seasoning, sprinkle with the chopped parsley and serve immediately, straight from the pan.

Nutritional information per portion: Energy 457kcal/1919kJ; Protein 39.2g; Carbohydrate 28.2g, of which sugars 16.4g; Fat 19.1g, of which saturates 3.7g; Cholesterol 42mg; Calcium 58mg; Fibre 4.4g; Sodium 100mg.

Vieiras de Santiago

SERVES 4

30ml/2 tbsp olive oil

1 onion, finely chopped

2 garlic cloves, finely chopped

200g/7oz can tomatoes

pinch of cayenne pepper

45ml/3 tbsp finely chopped fresh parsley

50ml/2fl oz/1/4 cup orange juice

50g/2oz/4 tbsp butter

450g/1lb large shelled scallops, or 8–12 large ones on the shell, detached and cleaned

30ml/2 tbsp anis spirit, such as Ricard or Pernod

90ml/6 tbsp stale breadcrumbs salt and ground black pepper

Instructions

Heat the oil in a pan and fry the onion and garlic over a gentle heat. Add the tomatoes and cook for 10–15 minutes, stirring occasionally. Season with a little salt and cayenne pepper. Transfer to a food processor or blender, add 30ml/2 tbsp of the parsley and the orange juice and blend to form a purée.

Preheat the grill (broiler) with the shelf at its highest. Arrange four curved scallop shells, or flameproof ramekin dishes, on a baking tray. Heat 25g/1oz/2 tbsp of the butter in a small frying pan and fry the scallops gently, for about 2 minutes, or until sealed but not totally cooked through.

Pour the anis into a ladle and set light to it. Pour over the scallops and shake the pan gently until the flames die down. Divide the scallops among the shells and salt them lightly. Add the pan juices to the tomato sauce.

Pour the tomato sauce over the scallops. Mix together the breadcrumbs and the remaining parsley, season very lightly and sprinkle over the top. Melt the remaining butter in a small pan and drizzle over the breadcrumbs. Grill (broil) the scallops for about 1 minute to heat through. Serve immediately.

Nutritional information per portion: Energy 394kcal/1652kJ; Protein 29.7g; Carbohydrate 25.5g, of which sugars 4.4g; Fat 18.1g, of which saturates 7.8g; Cholesterol 80mg; Calcium 95mg; Fibre 1.8g; Sodium 459mg.

Spinach with raisins and pine nuts

SERVES 4

50g/2oz/1/3 cup raisins, preferably Malaga raisins

1 thick slice white bread

45ml/3 tbsp olive oil

25g/1oz/1/4 cup pine nuts

500g/11/4lb young spinach, stalks removed

2 garlic cloves, finely chopped salt and ground black pepper

Instructions

Put the raisins in a small bowl and pour over enough boiling water to cover.

Leave the raisins to soak for about 10 minutes, then drain well.

Cut off the crusts from the white bread and cut into cubes. Heat 30ml/2 tbsp of the oil in a frying pan and fry the cubes of bread until golden. Drain.

Heat the remaining oil in the pan. Gently fry the pine nuts until just colouring. Add the spinach and garlic and cook quickly, turning the spinach until it has just wilted.

Add the raisins and season lightly with salt and pepper. Transfer to a warmed dish. Sprinkle with the croûtons and serve immediately.

Nutritional information per portion: Energy 206kcal/855kJ; Protein 5.8g; Carbohydrate 15.5g, of which sugars 11.1g; Fat 13.8g, of which saturates 1.6g; Cholesterol 0mg; Calcium 228mg; Fibre 3.4g; Sodium 218mg.

Zarzuela

SERVES 6

250g/9oz monkfish on the bone

1 gurnard, snapper or other whole white fish, about 350g/12oz, cleaned

1 sole, plaice or flounder or other whole flat fish, about 500g/1¼lb, cleaned

60ml/4 tbsp olive oil

8 small squid, with tentacles

plain (all-purpose) flour, for dusting

30ml/2 tbsp anis spirit, such as Ricard or Pernod

250ml/8fl oz/1 cup white wine 450g/1lb mussels, cleaned

4 large raw scampi (extra large shrimp), with heads

12 raw king prawns (jumbo shrimp), with heads

115g/4oz raw shelled prawns (shrimp)

salt and ground black pepper

45ml/3 tbsp chopped fresh parsley, to garnish

FOR THE STOCK

1 onion, chopped

1 celery stick, chopped

1 bay leaf

FOR THE FISH BROTH

30ml/2 tbsp oil

1 large onion, finely chopped

2 garlic cloves, finely chopped

500g/11/4lb ripe tomatoes, peeled, seeded and chopped

2 bay leaves

1 dried chilli, seeded and chopped

5ml/1 tsp paprika

pinch of saffron threads (0.2g)

salt and ground black pepper

Instructions

Prepare the fish. Remove the flesh from the bones and cut into portions. You should have about 500g/11/4lb white fish, both firm and soft. Salt the fish and reserve on a plate in the refrigerator. (Reserve the bones and heads for making the stock.)

Make the stock. Put the onion, celery, bay leaf and the fish bones and heads in a pan, pour in 600ml/1 pint/21/2 cups water, and bring to the boil, then simmer for about 30 minutes.

Make the broth in a large, heavy pan. Heat the oil and fry the onion and garlic gently until soft. Add the chopped tomatoes, bay leaves, dried chilli, paprika and crumbled saffron and cook gently to make a sauce.

To cook the fish and shellfish, heat the oil in a large frying pan. Put in the squid tentacles, face down, and cook for 45 seconds, to make "flowers". Reserve on a plate.

Flour and fry the monkfish and white fish for 3 minutes on each side, then the flat fish for 2 minutes on each side. Cut the squid bodies into rings and fry. Pour the anis spirit into a ladle, flame it and pour over the fish remaining in the pan. Remove the fish and reserve.

Strain the fish stock into the tomato sauce and add the wine. Bring to a simmer. Add the mussels in two batches. Cover for a couple of minutes, then remove to a plate, discard any closed mussels, and remove the upper shells.

Add the scampi and cook for about 8 minutes, then lift out using a slotted spoon. Cut with scissors along the underside from the head to the tail. Add the raw king prawns for 3–4 minutes, then lift out and reserve.

About 20 minutes before serving, assemble the casserole. Add the seafood to the hot broth in the following order, bringing the liquid back to simmering each time: firm white fish, soft white fish (with squid rings and pan juices), large shellfish in the shell, cooked shellfish in the shell, then any small shelled prawns. If the liquid level falls below the seafood, make it up with more wine. Check the seasonings.

Rearrange the soup with the best-looking shellfish and squid flowers on top. Scatter over the mussels, cover and leave to steam for 2 minutes. Garnish with parsley and serve.

Nutritional information per portion: Energy 326kcal/1367kJ; Protein 34.8g; Carbohydrate 5.4g, of which sugars 3.4g; Fat 14.4g, of which saturates 2.3g; Cholesterol 248mg; Calcium 79mg; Fibre 1g; Sodium 264mg.

Braised cabbage with chorizo

SERVES 4

50g/2oz/1/4 cup butter

5ml/1 tsp coriander seeds

225g/8oz green cabbage, shredded

2 garlic cloves, finely chopped

50g/2oz cured chorizo sausage, roughly chopped

60ml/4 tbsp dry sherry or white wine salt and ground black pepper

Instructions

Melt the butter in a large frying pan, add the coriander seeds and cook for 1 minute. Add the shredded cabbage to the pan with the chopped garlic and chorizo. Stir-fry gently for 5 minutes.

Add the sherry or wine and plenty of salt and pepper to the pan. Cover and cook for 15–20 minutes until the cabbage is tender. Check the seasoning, adding more if necessary, and then serve.

Nutritional information per portion: Energy 163kcal/673kJ; Protein 2.1g; Carbohydrate 4.6g, of which sugars 3.3g; Fat 13.4g, of which saturates 7.8g; Cholesterol 32mg; Calcium 37mg; Fibre 1.3g; Sodium 183mg.

Escalivada

SERVES 4

2–3 courgettes (zucchini)

1 large fennel bulb

1 Spanish onion

2 large red (bell) peppers

450g/1lb butternut squash

6 whole garlic cloves, unpeeled

75ml/5 tbsp olive oil

juice of 1/2 lemon

pinch of cumin seeds, crushed

4 sprigs fresh thyme

4 medium tomatoes, halved

salt and ground black pepper

Instructions

Preheat the oven to 220°C/425°F/Gas 7. Cut the courgettes lengthways into four pieces. Cut the fennel into similar-sized wedges. Slice the onion lengthways into chunks. Halve and seed the peppers, and slice thickly lengthways. Cut the squash into thick chunks. Smash the garlic cloves with the flat of a knife, but leave the skins on.

Choose a roasting pan into which all the vegetables will fit in one layer. Put in all the vegetables except the tomatoes. Mix together the olive oil and lemon juice. Pour over the vegetables and toss them. Sprinkle with the cumin seeds, salt and pepper and tuck in the thyme sprigs. Roast for 20 minutes.

Gently stir the vegetables in the oil and add the tomatoes. Cook for a further 15 minutes, or until the vegetables are tender and slightly charred around the edges.

Nutritional information per portion: Energy 209kcal/864kJ; Protein 4.6g; Carbohydrate 14.3g, of which sugars 13g; Fat 15.1g, of which saturates 2.4g; Cholesterol 0mg; Calcium 86mg; Fibre 5.6g; Sodium 17mg.

Chilled avocado soup with cumin

SERVES 4

3 ripe avocados

1 bunch spring onions (scallions), white parts only, trimmed and roughly chopped

2 garlic cloves, chopped

juice of 1 lemon

1.5ml/1/4 tsp ground cumin

1.5ml/1/4 tsp paprika

450ml/3/4 pint/scant 2 cups fresh chicken stock, cooled, and all fat skimmed off

300ml/1/2 pint/11/4 cups iced water salt and ground black pepper chopped fresh flat leaf parsley, to serve

Instructions

Starting half a day ahead, put the flesh of one avocado in a food processor or blender. Add the spring onions, garlic and lemon juice and purée until smooth. Add the second avocado and purée, then the third, with the spices and seasoning.

Purée until smooth.

Gradually add the stock. Pour the soup into a bowl and chill it for several hours.

To serve, stir in the iced water, then season to taste with plenty of salt and black pepper. Garnish with chopped parsley and then serve.

Nutritional information per portion: Energy 151kcal/623kJ; Protein 2.1g; Carbohydrate 2.6g, of which sugars 1.1g; Fat 14.6g, of which saturates 3.1g; Cholesterol 0mg; Calcium 19mg; Fibre 3g; Sodium 6mg.

Ensaladilla

SERVES 4

8 new potatoes, scrubbed and quartered

1 large carrot, diced

115g/4oz fine green beans, cut into 2cm/3/4in lengths 75g/3oz/3/4 cup peas

1/2 Spanish onion, chopped

4 cornichons or small gherkins, sliced

1 small red (bell) pepper, seeded and diced

50g/2oz/1/2 cup pitted black olives

15ml/1 tbsp drained pickled capers

15ml/1 tbsp freshly squeezed lemon juice

30ml/2 tbsp chopped fennel or parsley

salt and ground black pepper

FOR THE AIOLI

2 garlic cloves, finely chopped

2.5ml/1/2 tsp salt

150ml/1/4 pint/2/3 cup mayonnaise

Ingredients

To make the aioli, crush the garlic with the salt in a mortar and whisk or stir into the mayonnaise.

Cook the potatoes and diced carrot in a pan of boiling lightly salted water for 5–8 minutes until almost tender. Add the beans and peas to the pan and cook for 2 minutes, or until all the vegetables are tender. Drain well.

Put the vegetables into a large bowl. Add the onion, cornichons or gherkins, red pepper, olives and capers. Stir in the aioli and season to taste with the black pepper and the lemon juice.

Toss the vegetables and aioli together until well combined, check the seasoning and chill well. Serve garnished with fennel or parsley.

Nutritional information per portion: Energy 494kcal/2045kJ; Protein 5.1g; Carbohydrate 25.6g, of which sugars 8.1g; Fat 42g, of which saturates 6.3g; Cholesterol 28mg; Calcium 60mg; Fibre 4.5g; Sodium 191mg.

Spicy sausage and cheese tortilla

SERVES 4–6

75ml/5 tbsp olive oil

175g/6oz frying chorizo or spicy sausage, thinly sliced

675g/1 1/2lb waxy potatoes, thinly sliced

2 Spanish onions, halved and thinly sliced

4 large (US extra large) eggs

30ml/2 tbsp chopped fresh parsley, plus extra to garnish

115g/4oz/1 cup grated Cheddar or other hard cheese salt and ground black pepper

Instructions

1 Heat 15ml/1 tbsp of the oil in a 23cm/9in frying pan and fry the sausage until golden and cooked through. Drain on kitchen paper.

Add a further 30ml/2 tbsp oil to the pan and fry the potatoes and onions for 2–3 minutes, turning frequently. Cover tightly and cook over a gentle heat for about 30 minutes, turning occasionally, until softened and slightly golden.

In a large mixing bowl, beat together the eggs, parsley, cheese, sausage and plenty of seasoning. Gently stir in the potatoes and onions until coated.

Wipe out the pan with kitchen paper and heat the remaining 30ml/2 tbsp oil. Add the potato mixture and cook, over a very low heat, until the egg begins to set. Use a metal spatula to prevent the tortilla sticking and to allow the uncooked egg to run underneath.

Preheat the grill (broiler) to high. When the base of the tortilla has set, which should take about 5 minutes, protect the pan handle with foil and place the tortilla under the grill until it is set and golden. Cut into wedges and serve garnished with parsley.

Nutritional information per portion: Energy 409kcal/1703kJ; Protein 14.9g; Carbohydrate 28.3g, of which sugars 6.8g; Fat 26.7g, of which saturates 9.5g; Cholesterol 157mg; Calcium 212mg; Fibre 2.7g; Sodium 438mg.

Calamares rellenos

SERVES 4

2 squid, about 275g/10oz each

60ml/4 tbsp olive oil

1 small onion, finely chopped

2 garlic cloves, finely chopped

50g/2oz Serrano ham or gammon steak, diced finely

75g/3oz/scant 1/2 cup long grain rice

30ml/2 tbsp raisins, chopped

30ml/2 tbsp finely chopped fresh parsley

1/2 small (US medium) egg, beaten

plain (all-purpose) flour, for dusting

250ml/8fl oz/1 cup white wine

1 bay leaf

30ml/2 tbsp chopped fresh parsley

salt, paprika and black pepper

FOR THE TOMATO SAUCE

30ml/2 tbsp olive oil

1 onion, finely chopped

2 garlic cloves, finely chopped

200g/7oz can tomatoes

salt and cayenne pepper

Instructions

Make the tomato sauce. Heat the oil in a heavy pan large enough to hold the squid. Gently fry the onion and garlic. Add the tomatoes and cook for 10–15 minutes. Season with salt and cayenne pepper.

To prepare the squid, use the tentacles to pull out the body. Cut off the tentacles, discarding the eyes and everything below. Flex the bodies to pop out the spinal structure. Chop the fin flaps and rinse the bodies well.

Heat half the oil in a pan and gently fry the onion and garlic together. Add the ham and squid tentacles and stir-fry. Off the heat stir in the rice, chopped raisins and parsley. Season well and add the egg to bind the ingredients.

Spoon the mixture into the squid bodies, then stitch each of them shut using a small skewer. Blot them with kitchen paper, then flour lightly. Heat the remaining oil in a pan and fry the squid, turning until coloured on all sides.

Arrange the squid in the tomato sauce. Add the wine and bay leaf. Cover the pan tightly and simmer for 30 minutes. Serve sliced into rings, surrounded by the sauce and garnished with parsley.

Nutritional information per portion: Energy 441kcal/1844kJ; Protein 28.8g; Carbohydrate 27g, of which sugars 9.4g; Fat 20.1g, of which saturates 3.2g; Cholesterol 346mg; Calcium 84mg; Fibre 2.1g; Sodium 364mg.

Pisto manchego

SERVES 4

45ml/3 tbsp olive oil

2 Spanish onions, thinly sliced

3 garlic cloves, finely chopped

3 large green (bell) peppers, seeded and chopped

3 large courgettes (zucchini), thinly sliced

5 large ripe tomatoes or 800g/13/4lb can tomatoes, with juice

60ml/4 tbsp chopped fresh parsley

2 hard-boiled eggs, chopped (optional)

30ml/2 tbsp extra virgin olive oil (if serving cold)

salt and ground black pepper

Instructions

Heat the oil in a large, heavy pan and cook the sliced onions and garlic gently, until they are soft.

Add the peppers, courgettes and tomatoes. Season and cook gently over a low heat for 20 minutes to blend the flavours.

Stir in 30ml/2 tbsp parsley and serve hot, if wished, topped with chopped hard-boiled egg, if using, and more parsley. To serve cold, check the seasoning, adding more if needed, and sprinkle with a little extra virgin olive oil before adding the parsley garnish.

Nutritional information per portion: Energy 196kcal/812kJ; Protein 6.2g; Carbohydrate 21.3g, of which sugars 18.5g; Fat 10g, of which saturates 1.6g; Cholesterol 0mg; Calcium 109mg; Fibre 6.4g; Sodium 25mg.

Scrambled eggs with spring asparagus

SERVES 4

1 bunch thin asparagus

30–45ml/2–3 tbsp mangetouts (snow peas)

8 large (US extra large) eggs

30ml/2 tbsp milk

50g/2oz/1/4 cup butter

salt and ground black pepper

sweet paprika, for dusting

Instructions

Prepare the asparagus. Using a sharp knife, cut off and discard any hard stems. Cut the stems, keeping the tips separate. Shell some of the fatter mangetout pods, to extract the peas, and cut the pods into strips, if you like.

Put the stems into a pan of boiling water and simmer for 4 minutes. Add the asparagus tips, and cook for another 6 minutes. If including some pea pod strips, cook them for 2 minutes. Break the eggs into a bowl and beat together with the milk, salt and black pepper.

Melt the butter in a frying pan and pour in the eggs, scrambling them by pulling the cooked outsides to the middle with a wooden spoon. When the eggs are almost cooked, drain the asparagus and pea pod strips, if using, and stir into the eggs. Sprinkle the peas over the top, dust with paprika and serve.

Nutritional information per portion: Energy 262kcal/1085kJ; Protein 14.9g; Carbohydrate 2.2g, of which sugars 1.4g; Fat 21.9g, of which saturates 9.7g; Cholesterol 407mg; Calcium 78mg; Fibre 1.4g; Sodium 217mg.

Olive and anchovy bites

MAKES 40–45

115g/4oz/1 cup plain (all-purpose) flour

115g/4oz/1/2 cup chilled butter, diced

115g/4oz/1 cup finely grated Manchego, mature (sharp) Cheddar or Gruyère cheese

50g/2oz can anchovy fillets in oil, drained and roughly chopped

50g/2oz/1/2 cup pitted black olives, roughly chopped

2.5ml/1/2 tsp cayenne pepper

sea salt, to serve (optional)

Instructions

Place the flour, butter, cheese, anchovies, olives and cayenne pepper in a food processor and pulse until the mixture forms a firm dough.

Wrap the dough loosely in clear film (plastic wrap). Chill in the refrigerator for 20 minutes.

Preheat the oven to 200°C/400°F/Gas 6. Remove the dough from the refrigerator, then roll it out thinly on a lightly floured surface.

Cut the dough into 5cm/2in wide strips, then cut across each strip in alternate directions, to make triangles. Transfer the triangles to baking sheets and bake for 8–10 minutes until golden. Cool on a wire rack. Sprinkle with sea salt, if desired.

Nutritional information per anchovy bite: Energy 42kcal/173kJ; Protein 1.2g; Carbohydrate 2g, of which sugars 0.1g; Fat 3.2g, of which saturates 1.9g; Cholesterol 9mg; Calcium 27mg; Fibre 0.1g; Sodium 103mg.

Gazpacho

SERVES 4

1.3–1.6kg/3–3 1/2lb ripe tomatoes

1 green (bell) pepper, seeded and roughly chopped

2 garlic cloves, finely chopped

2 slices stale bread, crusts removed

60ml/4 tbsp extra virgin olive oil

60ml/4 tbsp sherry vinegar

150ml/1/4 pint/2/3 cup tomato juice

300ml/1/2 pint/1 1/4 cups iced water

salt and ground black pepper

ice cubes, to serve (optional)

FOR THE GARNISHES

30ml/2 tbsp olive oil

2–3 slices stale bread, diced

1 small cucumber, peeled and finely diced

1 small onion, finely chopped

1 red and 1 green (bell) pepper, seeded and finely diced

2 hard-boiled eggs, chopped

Ingredients

Skin the tomatoes, then quarter them and remove the cores and seeds, saving the juices. Put the pepper in a food processor and process for a few seconds. Add the tomatoes, reserved juices, garlic, bread, oil and vinegar and process. Add the tomato juice and blend until it is combined.

Season the soup, then pour into a large bowl, cover with clear film (plastic wrap) and chill for at least 12 hours.

Prepare the garnishes. Heat the olive oil in a frying pan and fry the bread cubes for 4–5 minutes until golden brown and crisp. Drain well on kitchen paper, then arrange in a small dish. Place the remaining garnishes in separate small dishes.

Just before serving, dilute the soup with the ice-cold water. The consistency should be thick but not stodgy. If you like, stir a few ice cubes into the soup, then serve with the garnishes.

Nutritional information per portion: Energy 376kcal/1584kJ; Protein 11.3g; Carbohydrate 38.3g, of which sugars 31.3g; Fat 21.1g, of which saturates 3.6g; Cholesterol 95mg; Calcium 109mg; Fibre 8.3g; Sodium 103mg.

Mushroom, bean and chorizo salad

SERVES 4

225g/8oz shelled broad (fava) beans

175g/6oz frying chorizo

60ml/4 tbsp extra virgin olive oil

225g/8oz/3 cups brown cap (cremini) mushrooms, sliced

60ml/4 tbsp chopped fresh chives salt and ground black pepper

Ingredients

Cook the broad beans in a pan of salted boiling water for 7–8 minutes. Drain and refresh under cold water.

Remove the skin from the sausage. If it doesn't peel off easily, score along the length of the sausage with a sharp knife first. Cut the chorizo into small chunks. Heat the oil in a small pan, add the chorizo and cook for 2–3 minutes.

Put the sliced mushrooms in a bowl and add the chorizo and oil. Toss to combine then leave to cool.

If the beans are large, peel away the tough outer skins. Stir the beans and half the chives into the mushroom mixture, and season to taste. Serve at room temperature, garnished with the remaining chives.

Nutritional information per portion: Energy 166kcal/684kJ; Protein 1.4g; Carbohydrate 2.7g, of which sugars 0.9g; Fat 16.7g, of which saturates 2.4g; Cholesterol 0mg; Calcium 33mg; Fibre 1.3g; Sodium 46mg.

Spiced clams

SERVES 3–4

1 small onion, finely chopped

1 celery stick, sliced

2 garlic cloves, finely chopped

2.5cm/1in piece fresh root ginger, grated

30ml/2 tbsp olive oil

1.5ml/1/4 tsp chilli powder

5ml/1 tsp ground turmeric

30ml/2 tbsp chopped fresh parsley

500g/11/4lb small clams, in the shell

30ml/2 tbsp dry white wine

salt and ground black pepper

celery leaves, to garnish

fresh bread, to serve

Instructions

Place the onion, celery, garlic and ginger in a large pan, add the olive oil, spices and chopped parsley and stir-fry for about 5 minutes. Add the clams to the pan and cook for 2 minutes.

Add the wine, then cover and cook gently for 2–3 minutes, shaking the pan occasionally. Season. Discard any clams whose shells remain closed, then serve, garnished with the celery leaves.

COOK'S TIP

There are many varieties of clam. The almeja fina (carpet shell clam) is perfect for this dish. Before cooking, check that all the shells are closed, and discard any that do not close when tapped. Discard any clams that do not open after cooking.

Nutritional information per portion: Energy 92kcal/381kJ; Protein 6.5g; Carbohydrate 2.2g, of which sugars 1.1g; Fat 5.9g, of which saturates 0.9g; Cholesterol 25mg; Calcium 50mg; Fibre 0.7g; Sodium 458mg.

Flash-fried squid with paprika and garlic

SERVES 6–8

500g/1 1/4lb very small squid, cleaned

90ml/6 tbsp olive oil

1 fresh red chilli, seeded and finely chopped

10ml/2 tsp Spanish mild smoked paprika

30ml/2 tbsp plain (all-purpose) flour

2 garlic cloves, finely chopped

15ml/1 tbsp sherry vinegar

5ml/1 tsp grated lemon rind

30–45ml/2–3 tbsp finely chopped fresh parsley salt and ground black pepper

Instructions

Cut the squid body sacs into rings and cut the tentacles into pieces.

Place the squid in a bowl. Mix 30ml/2 tbsp of the olive oil with half the chilli, the paprika, salt and pepper, and pour over the squid. Cover with clear film (plastic wrap), then place in the refrigerator and leave to marinate for 2–4 hours.

Toss the squid in the flour and divide it into two batches. Heat the remaining oil in a wok or deep frying pan over a high heat until very hot. Add the first batch of squid and quickly stir-fry for 1–2 minutes, or until it becomes opaque and the tentacles curl.

Add half the garlic. Stir, then turn out into a bowl. Repeat with the second batch of squid, adding more oil if needed.

Sprinkle with the vinegar, lemon rind, remaining chilli and parsley. Season and serve either hot or cool.

Nutritional information per portion: Energy 139kcal/580kJ; Protein 10.1g; Carbohydrate 3.8g, of which sugars 0.1g; Fat 9.4g, of which saturates 1.4g; Cholesterol 141mg; Calcium 21mg; Fibre 0.3g; Sodium 70mg.

Buñuelos

SERVES 4

50g/2oz/1/4 cup butter, diced

1.5ml/1/4 tsp salt

250ml/8fl oz/1 cup water

115g/4oz/1 cup plain (all-purpose) flour

2 whole eggs, plus 1 yolk

2.5ml/1/2 tsp Dijon mustard

2.5ml/1/2 tsp cayenne pepper

50g/2oz/1/2 cup finely grated Manchego or Cheddar cheese

Instructions

Preheat the oven to 220°C/425°F/Gas 7. Place the butter and the salt in a pan, then add the water. Bring the liquid to the boil. Meanwhile, sift the flour on to a sheet of baking parchment or greaseproof (waxed) paper.

Working quickly, tip the flour into the pan of boiling liquid in one go and stir it in immediately. Beat the mixture vigorously with a wooden spoon until it forms a thick paste that binds together and leaves the sides of the pan clean. Remove the pan from the heat.

Gradually beat the eggs and yolk into the mixture, then add the mustard, cayenne pepper and cheese.

Place teaspoonfuls of mixture on a non-stick baking sheet and bake for 10 minutes. Reduce the temperature to 180°C/350°F/Gas 4. Cook for 15 minutes until well browned. Serve hot or cold.

Nutritional information per portion: Energy 296kcal/1235kJ; Protein 9.9g; Carbohydrate 22.5g, of which sugars 0.6g; Fat 18.9g, of which saturates 10.5g; Cholesterol 184mg; Calcium 156mg; Fibre 0.9g; Sodium 223mg.

Chicharrones

SERVES 4

115g/4oz pork rind

vegetable oil, for frying

paprika and coarse sea salt, for sprinkling

Instructions

Using a sharp knife, cut the pork rind into strips. There is no need to be too precise, but try to make the strips roughly 1cm/1/2in wide and 2.5cm/1in long.

Pour the vegetable oil to a depth of 2.5cm/1in in a deep, heavy frying pan. Heat the oil and check that it has reached the correct temperature by immersing a cube of bread, which should brown in 1 minute.

Cook the strips of rind in the oil for 1–2 minutes, until they are puffed up and golden brown. Remove with a slotted spoon and drain on kitchen paper.

Sprinkle the chicharrones with paprika and salt to taste. Serve them hot or cold. Although they are at their best 1–2 days after cooking, they will keep reasonably well for up to 2 weeks in an airtight container.

Nutritional information per portion: Energy 247kcal/1018kJ; Protein 4.1g; Carbohydrate 0g, of which sugars 0g; Fat 25g, of which saturates 6.4g; Cholesterol 28mg; Calcium 3mg; Fibre 0g; Sodium 20mg.

Flamenco eggs

SERVES 4

30ml/2 tbsp olive oil

115g/4oz smoked bacon lardons or diced pancetta

2 frying chorizos, cubed

1 onion, chopped

2 garlic cloves, finely chopped

1 red and 1 green (bell) pepper, seeded and chopped 500g/11/4lb tomatoes, chopped 15–30ml/1–2 tbsp fino sherry

45ml/3 tbsp chopped fresh parsley

8 large (US extra large) eggs

salt, paprika and cayenne

FOR THE MIGAS

4 thick slices stale bread

oil, for frying

2 garlic cloves, bruised

Instructions

Preheat the oven to 180°C/350°F/Gas 4. Warm four individual baking dishes.

Heat the oil in a frying pan and fry the bacon or pancetta and chorizos, to give off their fat. Add the onion and garlic and cook gently until softened, stirring. Add the peppers and tomatoes and cook until reduced, stirring occasionally. Add some paprika and sherry.

Divide the mixture evenly among the baking dishes. Sprinkle with parsley. Swirl the eggs together with a fork and season well with salt and cayenne. Pour over the mixture. Bake the eggs and vegetables for 8 minutes, or until the eggs are just set.

Meanwhile make the migas. Cut the crusts off the bread and reduce to crumbs in a food processor.

Heat plenty of oil in a frying pan over a high heat, add the garlic cloves for a few moments to flavour it, then discard them. Throw in the crumbs and brown quickly, scooping them out on to kitchen paper. Season with a little salt and paprika, then sprinkle around the edge of the eggs to serve.

Nutritional information per portion: Energy 592kcal/2464kJ; Protein 26.6g; Carbohydrate 30.4g, of which sugars 12g; Fat 41.1g, of which saturates 11.8g; Cholesterol 416mg; Calcium 155mg; Fibre 4.1g; Sodium 1150mg.

Rice tortitas

SERVES 4

30ml/2 tbsp olive oil

115g/4oz/1 cup cooked long grain white rice

1 potato, grated

4 spring onions (scallions), thinly sliced

1 garlic clove, finely chopped

15ml/1 tbsp chopped fresh parsley

3 large (US extra large) eggs, beaten

2.5ml/1/2 tsp paprika

salt and ground black pepper

Instructions

Heat half the olive oil in a large frying pan and stir-fry the rice, together with the potato, spring onions and garlic, over a high heat for 3 minutes until golden.

Put the rice and vegetable mixture into a bowl and stir in the parsley and eggs, with the paprika and plenty of salt and pepper. Mix well.

Heat the remaining oil in the frying pan and drop in large spoonfuls of the rice mixture, leaving space for spreading. Cook the tortitas for 1–2 minutes on each side until golden.

Drain the tortitas on kitchen paper and keep hot while cooking the remaining mixture. Serve hot.

Nutritional information per portion: Energy 185kcal/776kJ; Protein 6.8g; Carbohydrate 17.6g, of which sugars 1.2g; Fat 10.4g, of which saturates 2.1g; Cholesterol 143mg; Calcium 56mg; Fibre 1.3g; Sodium 63mg.

Sizzling prawns

SERVES 4

1–2 dried chillies (to taste)

60ml/4 tbsp olive oil

3 garlic cloves, finely chopped

16 large raw prawns (shrimp), in the shell

French bread, to serve

Instructions

Split the chillies lengthways and discard the seeds. It is best to do this with a knife and fork, because the inner membranes contain a lot of capsaicin, which can be irritating to the eyes, nose and mouth.

Heat the oil in a large frying pan and stir-fry the garlic and chilli for 1 minute, until the garlic begins to turn brown.

Add the whole prawns and stir-fry for 3–4 minutes, coating them well with the flavoured oil.

Remove from the heat and divide the prawns among four dishes. Spoon over the flavoured oil and serve immediately, with French bread. (Remember to provide a plate for the heads and shells, plus plenty of napkins for messy fingers.)

Nutritional information per portion: Energy 147kcal/607kJ; Protein 11g; Carbohydrate 0g, of which sugars 0g; Fat 11.4g, of which saturates 1.6g; Cholesterol 122mg; Calcium 50mg; Fibre 0g; Sodium 119mg.

King prawns in crispy batter

SERVES 4

120ml/4fl oz/1/2 cup water

1 large (US extra large) egg

115g/4oz/1 cup plain (all-purpose) flour

5ml/1 tsp cayenne pepper

12 raw king prawns (jumbo shrimp), in the shell vegetable oil, for deep-frying flat leaf parsley, to garnish

lemon wedges, to serve (optional)

Instructions

In a large bowl, whisk together the water and the egg. Whisk in the flour and cayenne pepper until the mixture is smooth.

Peel the prawns, leaving just the tails intact. Using a sharp knife, make a shallow cut down the back of each prawn.

Using the tip of the knife, carefully pull out and discard the dark intestinal tract.

Heat the oil in a large pan or deep-fryer, until a cube of bread dropped into the oil browns in 1 minute.

Holding the prawns by their tails, dip them into the batter, one at a time, shaking off any excess. Carefully drop each prawn into the oil and fry for 2–3 minutes until crisp and golden. Drain on kitchen paper, garnish with parsley and serve with lemon wedges, if you like.

Nutritional information per portion: Energy 253kcal/1061kJ; Protein 13.1g; Carbohydrate 22.4g, of which sugars 0.4g; Fat 13.1g, of which saturates 1.8g; Cholesterol 145mg; Calcium 87mg; Fibre 0.9g; Sodium 113mg.

Tapas of almonds, olives and cheese

SERVES 6–8

FOR THE MARINATED OLIVES

2.5ml/1/2 tsp coriander seeds

2.5ml/1/2 tsp fennel seeds

2 garlic cloves, crushed

5ml/1tsp chopped fresh rosemary

10ml/2 tsp chopped fresh parsley

15ml/1 tbsp sherry vinegar

30ml/2 tbsp olive oil

115g/4oz/2/3 cup black olives

115g/4oz/2/3 cup green olives

FOR THE MARINATED CHEESE

150g/5oz Manchego or other firm cheese

90ml/6 tbsp olive oil

15ml/1 tbsp white wine vinegar

5ml/1 tsp black peppercorns

1 garlic clove, sliced

fresh thyme or tarragon sprigs

fresh flat leaf parsley or tarragon sprigs, to garnish (optional)

FOR THE SALTED ALMONDS

1.5ml/1/4 tsp cayenne pepper

30ml/2 tbsp sea salt, plus extra for sprinkling (optional)

25g/1oz/2 tbsp butter

60ml/4 tbsp olive oil

200g/7oz/13/4 cups blanched almonds

Instructions

To make the marinated olives, crush the coriander and fennel seeds in a mortar with a pestle. Work in the garlic, then add the rosemary, parsley, vinegar and olive oil. Put the olives in a small bowl and pour over the marinade. Cover with clear film (plastic wrap) and chill for up to 1 week.

To make the marinated cheese, cut the cheese into bitesize pieces, removing any hard rind, and put in a small bowl. Combine the oil, vinegar, peppercorns, garlic and thyme or tarragon and pour over the cheese. Cover with clear film and chill for up to 3 days.

To make the salted almonds, combine the cayenne pepper and salt in a bowl. Melt the butter with the oil in a frying pan. Add the almonds and fry them, stirring, for 5 minutes, or until golden. Add the almonds to the salt mixture and toss until the almonds are coated. Leave to cool, then store in an airtight container for up to 1 week.

To serve, arrange the almonds, olives and cheese in three separate small, shallow dishes. Garnish the cheese with fresh herbs if you like and sprinkle the almonds with a little more salt, to taste.

Nutritional information per portion: Energy 432kcal/1784kJ; Protein 10.3g; Carbohydrate 1.8g, of which sugars 1.1g; Fat 42.3g, of which saturates 9.7g; Cholesterol 25mg; Calcium 217mg; Fibre 2.7g; Sodium 805mg.

Marinated anchovies

SERVES 4

225g/8oz fresh anchovies, heads and tails removed, and split open along the belly

juice of 3 lemons

30ml/2 tbsp extra virgin olive oil

2 garlic cloves, finely chopped

15ml/1 tbsp chopped fresh parsley

flaked sea salt

Instructions

Place the anchovies on a clean work surface and turn them on to their bellies, then press them down with your thumb.

Using the tip of a small, sharp knife, carefully remove the backbones from the flattened fish, and then arrange the anchovies skinside down in a single layer on a large plate.

Squeeze two-thirds of the lemon juice over the fish and sprinkle them with the salt. Cover and leave to stand for up to 24 hours, basting occasionally with the juices, until the flesh is white and no longer translucent.

Transfer the anchovies to a serving plate and drizzle with the olive oil and the remaining lemon juice. Sprinkle the fish with the chopped garlic and parsley, then cover with clear film (plastic wrap) and chill until ready to serve.

Nutritional information per portion: Energy 144kcal/597kJ; Protein 11.7g; Carbohydrate 0.1g, of which sugars 0.1g; Fat 10.7g, of which saturates 2.3g; Cholesterol 0mg; Calcium 55mg; Fibre 0.2g; Sodium 69mg.

Artichoke rice cakes with Manchego

SERVES 6

1 large globe artichoke

50g/2oz/1/4 cup butter

1 small onion, finely chopped

1 garlic clove, finely chopped

115g/4oz/2/3 cup paella rice

450ml/3/4 pint/scant 2 cups hot chicken stock 50g/2oz/2/3 cup freshly grated Parmesan cheese 150g/5oz Manchego cheese, very finely diced 45–60ml/3/4 tbsp fine corn meal olive oil, for frying

salt and ground black pepper

fresh flat leaf parsley, to garnish

Instructions

Remove the heart of the artichoke and chop finely.

Melt the butter in a pan and fry the artichoke heart, onion and garlic for 5 minutes. Add the rice and cook for 1 minute.

Keeping the heat fairly high, gradually add the stock, stirring until the liquid has been absorbed and the rice is cooked – this should take about 20 minutes. Season well, then stir in the Parmesan cheese. Transfer the mixture to a bowl. Cool, cover and chill for 2 hours.

Spoon about 15ml/1 tbsp of the mixture into the palm of one hand, flatten slightly, and place a few pieces of diced cheese in the centre. Shape the rice around the cheese to make a small ball. Flatten slightly, then roll in the corn meal, shaking off any excess. Repeat with the remaining mixture to make 12 rice cakes.

Shallow fry the rice cakes in hot olive oil for 4–5 minutes until they are crisp and golden brown. Drain the rice cakes on kitchen paper and serve hot, garnished with flat leaf parsley.

Nutritional information per portion: Energy 354kcal/1469kJ; Protein 12g; Carbohydrate 21.8g, of which sugars 0.8g; Fat 23.6g, of which saturates 12.3g; Cholesterol 50mg; Calcium 299mg; Fibre 0.5g; Sodium 331mg.

Stewed aubergine

SERVES 4

1 large aubergine (eggplant)

60–90ml/4–6 tbsp olive oil

2 shallots, thinly sliced

4 tomatoes, quartered

2 garlic cloves, thinly sliced

60ml/4 tbsp red wine

30ml/2 tbsp chopped fresh parsley, plus extra to garnish

30–45ml/2–3 tbsp extra virgin olive oil (if serving cold) salt and ground black pepper

Ingredients

Slice the aubergine into 1cm/1/2in rounds. Place them in a large colander and sprinkle with 5–10ml/1–2 tsp salt. Leave to drain for 30 minutes.

Rinse the aubergine slices well, then press between several layers of kitchen paper to remove any excess liquid.

Heat 30ml/2 tbsp of the oil in a large frying pan until smoking. Add a single layer of aubergine slices and fry, turning once, until golden brown. Remove to a plate covered with kitchen paper to drain. Heat more oil and fry the second batch in the same way.

Heat 15ml/1 tbsp of oil in a pan and cook the shallots for 5 minutes until golden. Cut the aubergine into strips. Add, with the tomatoes, garlic and wine. Cover and simmer for 30 minutes.

Stir in the parsley, and check the seasonings. Sprinkle with a little more parsley and serve hot. To serve cold, dribble a little extra virgin olive oil over the dish before it goes on the table.

Nutritional information per portion: Energy 197kcal/816kJ; Protein 2g; Carbohydrate 7.3g, of which sugars 6.7g; Fat 17.3g, of which saturates 2.6g; Cholesterol 0mg; Calcium 23mg; Fibre 3.5g; Sodium 15mg.

Sopa de mariscos

SERVES 4

675g/1 1/2lb raw prawns (shrimp), in the shell

900ml/1 1/2 pints/3 3/4 cups cold water

1 onion, chopped

1 celery stick, chopped

1 bay leaf

45ml/3 tbsp olive oil

2 slices stale bread, crusts removed

1 small onion, finely chopped

1 large garlic clove, chopped

2 large tomatoes, halved

1/2 large green (bell) pepper, finely chopped

500g/1 1/4lb cockles (small clams) or mussels, cleaned juice of 1 lemon

45ml/3 tbsp chopped fresh parsley

5ml/1 tsp paprika

salt and ground black pepper

Instructions

Pull the heads off the prawns and put them in a pan with the cold water. Add the onion, celery and bay leaf and simmer for 20–25 minutes. Peel the prawns, adding the shells to the stock.

Heat the oil in a large pan and fry the bread slices quickly, then reserve them. Fry the onion until it is soft, adding the garlic towards the end.

Scoop the seeds out of the tomatoes and discard. Chop the flesh and add to the pan with the green pepper. Fry briefly, stirring occasionally. Strain the stock into the pan and bring to the boil. Check over the cockles or mussels, discarding any that are open or damaged.

Add half the cockles or mussels to the stock. When open, transfer some of them out on to a plate. Remove the mussels or cockles from the shells and discard the shells. (You should end up having discarded about half of the shells.) Meanwhile, repeat the process to cook the remaining cockles or mussels.

Return the cockles or mussels to the soup and add the prawns. Add the bread, torn into little pieces, and the lemon juice and chopped parsley. Season to taste with paprika, salt and pepper and stir gently to mix in the bread. Serve.

Nutritional information per portion: Energy 301kcal/1266kJ; Protein 39.5g; Carbohydrate 13.5g, of which sugars 6.3g; Fat 10.3g, of which saturates 1.6g; Cholesterol 362mg; Calcium 223mg; Fibre 1.9g; Sodium 709mg.

Tortilla with beans

SERVES 2

45ml/3 tbsp olive oil

2 Spanish onions, thinly sliced 300g/11oz waxy potatoes, cut into dice

250g/9oz/13/4 cups shelled broad (fava) beans

5ml/1 tsp chopped fresh thyme or summer savory

6 large (US extra large) eggs

45ml/3 tbsp mixed chopped fresh chives and fresh flat leaf parsley salt and ground black pepper

Instructions

Heat 30ml/2 tbsp of the oil in a 23cm/9in deep non-stick frying pan. Add the onions and potatoes and stir to coat. Cover and cook gently, stirring, for 20–25 minutes until the potatoes are cooked.

Meanwhile, cook the beans in a pan of boiling salted water for 5 minutes.

Drain and set aside to cool.

When the beans are cool enough to handle, peel off and discard the grey outer skins. Add the beans to the frying pan, together with the thyme or summer savory, and season to taste. Stir well to mix and cook for a further 2–3 minutes.

Beat the eggs with salt and pepper to taste and add the mixed herbs, then pour over the potatoes and onions and increase the heat. Cook gently for 5 minutes, or until the bottom browns. During cooking, pull the tortilla away from the sides of the pan and tilt it to allow the uncooked egg to run underneath.

Cover the pan with a plate and invert the tortilla on to it. Add the remaining oil to the pan and heat. Slip the tortilla back into the pan, uncooked side down, and cook for 3–5 minutes until the underneath turns brown. Slide the tortilla out on to a plate. Cut it up and serve warm.

Nutritional information per portion: Energy 637kcal/2662kJ; Protein 33.7g; Carbohydrate 51.3g, of which sugars 12.5g; Fat 35g, of which saturates 7.3g; Cholesterol 571mg; Calcium 247mg; Fibre 12.9g; Sodium 249mg.

Chicken with lemon and garlic

SERVES 2–4

2 skinless chicken breast fillets

30ml/2 tbsp olive oil

1 shallot, finely chopped

4 garlic cloves, finely chopped

5ml/1 tsp paprika

juice of 1 lemon

30ml/2 tbsp chopped fresh parsley

salt and ground black pepper

fresh flat leaf parsley, to garnish

lemon wedges, to serve

Instructions

Remove the little fillet from the back of each breast. If the breast still looks fatter than a finger, bat it with a rolling pin to make it thinner. Slice all the chicken meat into strips.

Heat the oil in a large frying pan. Stir-fry the chicken strips with the shallot, garlic and paprika over a high heat for about 3 minutes until cooked through.

Add the lemon juice and parsley and season with salt and pepper to taste.

Serve hot with lemon wedges, garnished with flat leaf parsley.

Nutritional information per portion: Energy 138kcal/579kJ; Protein 18.5g; Carbohydrate 1.5g, of which sugars 1.1g; Fat 6.5g, of which saturates 1g; Cholesterol 53mg; Calcium 30mg; Fibre 0.8g; Sodium 49mg.

Avocado, orange and almond salad

SERVES 4

2–3 oranges

2 ripe tomatoes

2 small avocados

60ml/4 tbsp extra virgin olive oil

30ml/2 tbsp lemon juice

15ml/1 tbsp chopped fresh parsley

1 small onion, cut into rings

25g/1oz/1/4 cup split, toasted almonds

10–12 black olives

salt and ground black pepper

Instructions

Peel the oranges and slice them into thick rounds. Plunge the tomatoes into boiling water for 30 seconds, then refresh in cold water. Peel away the skins, cut the tomatoes into quarters, remove the seeds and chop them roughly. Cut the avocados in half, remove the stones (pits) and carefully peel away the skin. Cut into chunks.

Mix together the olive oil, lemon juice and parsley. Season with salt and pepper, then toss the avocados and tomatoes in half of the dressing.

Arrange the oranges on a plate and add the onion rings. Drizzle with the remaining dressing. Spoon over avocados, tomatoes, almonds and olives and serve.

Nutritional information per portion: Energy 295kcal/1224kJ; Protein 4g; Carbohydrate 12.5g, of which sugars 11.6g; Fat 25.8g, of which saturates 4.2g; Cholesterol 0mg; Calcium 85mg; Fibre 5g; Sodium 295mg.

Scrambled eggs with prawns

SERVES 4

1 bunch spring onions (scallions)

25g/1oz/2 tbsp butter

30ml/2 tbsp oil

150g/5oz shelled prawns (shrimp)

8 large (US extra large) eggs

30ml/2 tbsp milk

45ml/3 tbsp chopped fresh parsley

salt and ground black pepper

crusty bread, to serve

Instructions

Chop the white of the spring onions and reserve, keeping it separate from 30ml/2 tbsp of the green tops.

Heat the butter and oil in a large frying pan. Add the spring onion white and cook briefly. Add the prawns and heat through. (If the prawns are raw, then cook them for 2 minutes.)

Beat the eggs with the milk and then season. Turn the heat to medium-high and pour the egg mixture over the prawns. Cook for about 2 minutes, stirring with a wooden spoon.

Sprinkle with parsley and spring onion greens. Divide among four plates and serve immediately with crusty bread.

Nutritional information per portion: Energy 285kcal/1182kJ; Protein 20.2g; Carbohydrate 1.5g, of which sugars 1.4g; Fat 22.4g, of which saturates 7.3g; Cholesterol 467mg; Calcium 129mg; Fibre 1g; Sodium 258mg.

Charred artichokes with lemon oil dip

SERVES 2–4

15ml/1 tbsp lemon juice or white wine vinegar

2 globe artichokes

45ml/3 tbsp olive oil

sea salt

sprigs of fresh flat leaf parsley, to garnish

FOR THE LEMON OIL DIP

12 garlic cloves, unpeeled

1 lemon

45ml/3 tbsp extra virgin olive oil

Instructions

Preheat the oven to 200°C/400°F/Gas 6. Stir the lemon juice or the vinegar into a bowl of cold water.

Cut each artichoke lengthways into wedges. Pull the hairy choke out from the centre of each wedge and drop the wedges into the acidulated water.

Drain the artichokes and place in a roasting pan with the garlic cloves. Toss in the oil. Sprinkle with salt and roast for 40 minutes, stirring once or twice, until the artichokes are tender.

Meanwhile, make the dip. Pare away two strips of rind from the lemon and scrape away any pith. Place the rind in a pan with water to cover. Simmer for 5 minutes, then drain, refresh in cold water and chop roughly.

Arrange the artichokes on a plate and set aside to cool for 5 minutes. Flatten the garlic cloves so that the flesh pops out of the skins. Transfer the garlic flesh to a bowl, mash to a purée then add the lemon rind. Squeeze the juice from the lemon, then, using a fork, whisk in the olive oil and lemon juice.

Serve the artichokes warm, garnished with the parsley and accompanied with the dip.

Nutritional information per portion: Energy 166kcal/684kJ; Protein 1.4g; Carbohydrate 2.7g, of which sugars 0.9g; Fat 16.7g, of which saturates 2.4g; Cholesterol 0mg; Calcium 33mg; Fibre 1.3g; Sodium 46mg.

San Esteban canelones

SERVES 4–8

60ml/4 tbsp olive oil

1 onion, finely chopped

1 carrot, finely chopped

2 garlic cloves, finely chopped

2 ripe tomatoes, peeled and finely chopped

25g/1oz/2 tbsp butter

150g/5oz raw chicken livers or cooked stuffing, diced

150g/5oz raw pork or cooked ham, gammon or sausage, diced

250g/9oz raw or cooked chicken, diced

5ml/1 tsp fresh thyme leaves

30ml/2 tbsp brandy

90ml/6 tbsp crème fraîche or double (heavy) cream

16 no pre-cook cannelloni tubes

75g/3oz/1 cup freshly grated Parmesan cheese salt and ground black pepper green salad, to serve

FOR THE WHITE SAUCE

50g/2oz/1/4 cup butter

50g/2oz/1/2 cup plain (all-purpose) flour

900ml/11/2 pints/33/4 cups milk freshly grated nutmeg, to taste

Instructions

Heat the oil in a large frying pan, add the onion, carrot, garlic and tomatoes and cook over a low heat, stirring, for about 10 minutes or until very soft.

Add the butter, then the raw meat, to the pan and cook until coloured. Add the remaining meats and sprinkle first with thyme, then with the brandy. Stir, then warm through and reduce the liquid.

Pour in the crème fraîche or cream, season to taste and leave to simmer for about 10 minutes. Cool briefly.

Preheat the oven to 190°C/375°F/Gas 5. Melt the butter in a pan, add the flour and cook, stirring, for 1–2 minutes. Gradually stir in the milk, a little at a time. Bring to simmering point, stirring until the sauce is smooth. Grate in nutmeg to taste, then season with plenty of salt and black pepper.

Spoon a little of the white sauce into a baking dish. Fill the cannelloni tubes with the meat mixture and arrange in a single layer in the dish. Pour the remaining white sauce over them, then sprinkle with the Parmesan cheese. Bake in the oven for 35–40 minutes, or until the pasta is tender. Leave for 10 minutes before serving with green salad.

Nutritional information per portion: Energy 480kcal/2014kJ; Protein 27.4g; Carbohydrate 40.5g, of which sugars 8.9g; Fat 23.5g, of which saturates 11.4g; Cholesterol 148mg; Calcium 282mg; Fibre 1.9g; Sodium 473mg.

Paella Valenciana

SERVES 6–8

90ml/6 tbsp white wine

450g/1lb fresh mussels, scrubbed

115g/4oz/scant

1 cup small shelled broad (fava) beans

150g/5oz green beans, cut into short lengths

90ml/6 tbsp olive oil

6 small skinless, boneless chicken breast portions, cut into large pieces

150g/5oz pork fillet, cubed

6–8 large raw prawn (shrimp) tails, deveined, or 12 smaller raw prawns

2 onions, chopped

2–3 garlic cloves, finely chopped

1 red (bell) pepper, seeded and sliced

2 ripe tomatoes, peeled, seeded and chopped

60ml/4 tbsp chopped fresh parsley

900ml/1½ pints/3¾ cups chicken stock

pinch of saffron threads (0.25g), soaked in 30ml/2 tbsp hot water

350g/12oz/1¾ cups paella rice, washed and drained

225g/8oz frying chorizo, sliced

115g/4oz/1 cup peas

6–8 stuffed green olives, sliced

salt, paprika and black pepper

Instructions

Heat the wine and add the mussels, discarding any that do not close when tapped. Cover and steam until opened. Reserve the liquid and mussels separately, discarding any that do not open.

Briefly cook the broad beans and green beans in boiling water, then drain. Pop the broad beans out of their skins.

Heat 45ml/3 tbsp oil in a large paella pan or wide flameproof casserole. Season the chicken with salt and paprika and fry, turning until browned on all sides. Reserve on a plate. Season the pork with salt and paprika. Add 15ml/1 tbsp oil and fry the seasoned pork until evenly browned. Reserve with the chicken. Fry the prawns briefly in the same pan, but reserve them separately.

Add the remaining oil to the pan and heat. Fry the onions and garlic for 3–4 minutes until golden brown. Add the red pepper, cook for 2–3 minutes, then stir in the chopped tomatoes and parsley and cook until thickened. If cooking in the oven, preheat to 190°C/375°F/Gas 5.

Stir the chicken stock, the reserved mussel liquid and the saffron liquid into the vegetables. Season well with salt and pepper and bring the mixture to the boil. When the liquid is bubbling, throw in all the rice. Stir once, then add the chicken pieces, pork, prawns, beans, chorizo and peas.

Transfer the pan to the oven and cook for 15–18 minutes until the rice is done. Alternatively, cook over medium-high heat for about 10 minutes. Then lower the heat and start to move the pan. A big pan needs to shift every 2–3 minutes, moving the edge of the pan round over the heat, then back to the centre. Cook until the rice is done – another 10–12 minutes.

Arrange the mussels and olives on top. Cover with a lid (or damp dishtowel) and leave to stand for 10 minutes, until all the liquid is absorbed. Serve straight from the pan.

COOK'S TIP

Traditionally, paella is cooked outdoors on a wide bed of hot charcoal. Indoors a big heat source such as a large hotplate or an oven is needed. Without this steady heat, the pan needs to be moved to cook the rice evenly.

Nutritional information per portion: Energy 712kcal/2978kJ; Protein 69.9g; Carbohydrate 48g, of which sugars 5.8g; Fat 26.1g, of which saturates 6.4g; Cholesterol 208mg; Calcium 98mg; Fibre 3.6g; Sodium 468mg.

Simple rice salad

SERVES 6

275g/10oz/1 1/2 cups long grain rice

1 bunch spring onions (scallions), finely sliced

1 green (bell) pepper, seeded and finely diced

1 yellow (bell) pepper, seeded and finely diced

225g/8oz tomatoes, peeled, seeded and chopped

30ml/2 tbsp chopped fresh flat leaf parsley or coriander (cilantro)

FOR THE DRESSING

75ml/5 tbsp extra virgin olive oil

15ml/1 tbsp sherry vinegar

5ml/1 tsp strong Dijon mustard

salt and ground black pepper

Instructions

Cook the rice in a large pan of lightly salted boiling water for 10–12 minutes, until tender but still al dente. Be careful not to overcook it.

Drain the rice well in a sieve (strainer), rinse thoroughly under cold running water and drain again. Leave the rice to cool completely.

Place the rice in a large serving bowl. Add the spring onions, peppers, tomatoes and parsley or coriander.

Make the dressing. Place all the ingredients in a screw-top jar, put the lid on and shake vigorously until well mixed. Stir the dressing into the rice and check the seasoning.

Nutritional information per portion: Energy 280kcal/1166kJ; Protein 4.9g; Carbohydrate 42.3g, of which sugars 5.5g; Fat 10g, of which saturates 1.4g; Cholesterol 0mg; Calcium 40mg; Fibre 2g; Sodium 34mg.

Pimiento tartlets

SERVES 4

1 red (bell) pepper

1 yellow (bell) pepper

175g/6oz/1 1/2 cups plain (all-purpose) flour

75g/3oz/6 tbsp chilled butter, diced

30–45ml/2–3 tbsp cold water

60ml/4 tbsp double (heavy) cream

1 egg

15ml/1 tbsp freshly grated Parmesan cheese salt and ground black pepper

Instructions

Preheat the oven to 200°C/400°F/Gas 6, and heat the grill (broiler). Place the peppers on a baking sheet and grill (broil) the peppers for 10 minutes, turning occasionally until blackened. Cover and leave for 5 minutes. Peel off skin, discard the seeds and cut the flesh into strips.

Sift the flour and a pinch of salt into a bowl. Rub in the butter until the mixture resembles fine breadcrumbs. Stir in enough water to make a firm, but not sticky, dough.

Roll the dough out thinly on a lightly floured surface and line 12 individual moulds or a 12-hole tartlet tin (muffin pan). Prick the bases with a fork and fill the cases with crumpled foil. Bake for 10 minutes. Remove the foil from the pastry cases and divide the pepper strips among the pastry cases.

Whisk the cream and egg in a bowl. Season and pour over the peppers. Sprinkle each tartlet with cheese and bake for 15–20 minutes until firm. Cool for 2 minutes, then transfer to a wire rack. Serve the tartlets warm or cold.

Nutritional information per portion: Energy 427kcal/1778kJ; Protein 8.4g; Carbohydrate 40g, of which sugars 6.4g; Fat 27g, of which saturates 16.1g; Cholesterol 112mg; Calcium 131mg; Fibre 2.8g; Sodium 180mg.

Andrajos

SERVES 6

800g/1 3/4lb hare meat and bone (the front legs and rib end)

200ml/7fl oz/scant

1 cup red wine 120–150ml/4–5fl oz/1/2–2/3 cup olive oil

150g/5oz bacon lardons, or diced pancetta 2 onions, chopped

2 large garlic cloves, finely chopped

8 baby onions, peeled

4 carrots, diced

4 chicken thighs, halved along the bone and seasoned seasoned plain (all-purpose) flour, for dusting

350g/12oz small open-cap mushrooms

600ml/1 pint/2 1/2 cups stock

5ml/1 tsp dried thyme

1 bay leaf

250g/9oz dried lasagne sheets

90ml/6 tbsp chopped fresh parsley

30ml/2 tbsp pine nuts

salt and ground black pepper

Instructions

Starting at least two days ahead, cut the hare into portions and put in a bowl. Pour over the red wine and 15ml/1 tbsp of the oil and leave to marinate in the refrigerator for at least 24 hours.

Heat 30ml/2 tbsp olive oil in a large, heavy pan, add the bacon or pancetta, chopped onions and garlic and fry until the onions are translucent. Halfway through add the whole baby onions and diced carrots, and continue cooking, stirring occasionally.

Heat 45ml/3 tbsp oil in a large frying pan and fry the seasoned chicken pieces on both sides until golden brown. Add to the onion mixture.

Remove the hare from the red wine marinade, reserving the liquid. Blot the meat well on kitchen paper and dredge with the seasoned flour until well coated. Add more oil to the frying pan, if necessary, and fry the meat on all sides until browned.

Meanwhile, reserve eight of the smallest open-cap mushrooms. Quarter the remaining mushrooms and add to the chicken mixture. Continue cooking the hare in the frying pan, stirring every now and then, until browned.

When the hare is ready, arrange the pieces in the pan. Pour the reserved marinade into the frying pan to deglaze it, then pour the juices into the pan.

Add the stock, dried thyme and bay leaf and season with salt and pepper. Cook over a low heat for 11/2 hours, until the meat is tender. Leave to cool.

When ready to serve, bring plenty of water to the boil in a large roasting pan with 5ml/1 tsp salt and 15ml/1 tbsp oil. Break up the lasagne sheets and spread out the pieces in the pan. Cook for 7–8 minutes until soft, moving the pieces around to prevent them from sticking.

Remove all the meat from the bones and return to the pan with 60ml/4 tbsp of the parsley. Bring to a simmer. Stir the drained pasta into the sauce. Heat 15ml/1 tbsp oil in a small pan and fry the reserved mushrooms, then arrange them on top. Sprinkle with the remaining parsley and the pine nuts, and serve.

Nutritional information per portion: Energy 589kcal/2464kJ; Protein 42.4g; Carbohydrate 38g, of which sugars 7g; Fat 28.3g, of which saturates 6.2g; Cholesterol 152mg; Calcium 75mg; Fibre 3.5g; Sodium 430mg.

Orange chicken salad

SERVES 4

3 large seedless oranges

175g/6oz/scant 1 cup long grain rice

175ml/6fl oz/3/4 cup vinaigrette

10ml/2 tsp strong Dijon mustard

2.5ml/1/2 tsp caster (superfine) sugar

450g/1lb cooked chicken, diced

45ml/3 tbsp chopped fresh chives

75g/3oz/3/4 cup almonds or cashew nuts, toasted

salt and ground black pepper

mixed salad leaves, to serve

Instructions

Pare one of the oranges thinly, removing only the rind, not the pith. Put the pieces of orange rind in a pan and add the rice. Pour in 475ml/16fl oz/2 cups water, add a pinch of salt and bring to the boil. Cover and cook over a very low heat for 15 minutes, or until the rice is tender and the water has been absorbed.

Meanwhile, peel the oranges, removing all the pith. Separate them into segments over a plate. Add the orange juice from the plate to the vinaigrette with the mustard and sugar, whisking to combine. Check the seasoning.

Discard the pieces of orange rind. from the cooked rice. Spoon the rice into a bowl, let it cool slightly, then add half the dressing. Toss well, then set aside to cool completely.

Add the chicken, chives, nuts and orange segments to the rice. Pour over the remaining dressing and toss. Serve on a bed of salad leaves.

Nutritional information per portion: Energy 642kcal/2678kJ; Protein 35.6g; Carbohydrate 49.5g, of which sugars 14g; Fat 33.7g, of which saturates 4.7g; Cholesterol 79mg; Calcium 118mg; Fibre 3.5g; Sodium 278mg.

Cuban-style rice

SERVES 4

3 garlic cloves

120ml/4fl oz/1/2 cup olive oil

300g/11oz/1 1/2 cups long grain rice

15g/1/2oz/1 tbsp butter

4 small bananas or 2 large bananas

4 large (US extra large) eggs

salt and paprika

FOR THE TOMATO SAUCE

30ml/2 tbsp olive oil

1 onion, chopped

2 garlic cloves, finely chopped

800g/1lb 12oz can tomatoes

4 thyme or oregano sprigs

ground black pepper

Instructions

Make the tomato sauce. Heat the oil in a pan, add the onion and garlic and fry gently, stirring, until soft. Stir in the tomatoes and thyme or oregano and simmer for 5 minutes. Add the seasoning. Remove the herbs and keep warm.

Put 850ml/1 pint 8fl oz/3 1/2 cups water in a pan with two whole garlic cloves and 15ml/1 tbsp oil. Bring to the boil, add the rice and cook for 18 minutes until it is done, and the liquid has been absorbed.

Heat a pan with 30ml/2 tbsp oil and gently fry one chopped garlic clove. Add the rice, stir, season well, then turn off the heat and cover the pan.

Heat the butter in a frying pan with 15ml/1 tbsp oil. Halve the bananas lengthways and fry briefly on both sides. Keep them warm.

Add 60ml/4 tbsp oil to the pan and fry the eggs over a medium-high heat, until the edges turn golden. Season to taste with salt and paprika. Serve the rice surrounded by the tomato sauce, bananas and fried eggs.

Nutritional information per portion: Energy 668kcal/2781kJ; Protein 13.9g; Carbohydrate 76.6g, of which sugars 15.4g; Fat 34g, of which saturates 7.2g; Cholesterol 198mg; Calcium 64mg; Fibre 2.7g; Sodium 112mg.

Sopa Castiliana

SERVES 4

30ml/2 tbsp olive oil

4 large garlic cloves, peeled

4 slices stale country bread

20ml/4 tsp paprika

1 litre/13/4 pints/4 cups beef stock

1.5ml/1/4 tsp ground cumin

4 eggs

salt and ground black pepper

chopped fresh parsley, to garnish

Instructions

Preheat the oven to 230°C/450°F/Gas 8. Heat the olive oil in a large pan. Add the whole peeled garlic cloves and cook gently until they are golden, then remove and set aside. Fry the slices of bread in the oil until they are golden, then set these aside.

Add 15ml/1 tbsp of the paprika to the pan, and fry for a few seconds. Stir in the beef stock, cumin and remaining paprika, then add the reserved garlic, crushing the cloves with the back of a wooden spoon. Season to taste, then cook for about 5 minutes.

Break up the slices of fried bread into bitesize pieces and stir them into the soup. Ladle the soup into four ovenproof bowls. Carefully break an egg into each bowl of soup and place in the oven for about 3 minutes, until the eggs are set. Sprinkle the soup with chopped fresh parsley and serve immediately.

Nutritional information per portion: Energy 208kcal/870kJ; Protein 9.5g; Carbohydrate 16.5g, of which sugars 0.8g; Fat 12.3g, of which saturates 2.4g; Cholesterol 190mg; Calcium 71mg; Fibre 0.5g; Sodium 228mg.

Catalan broad bean and potato soup

SERVES 4

30ml/2 tbsp olive oil

2 onions, chopped

3 large floury potatoes, peeled and diced

450g/1lb fresh shelled broad (US fava) beans, plus extra to garnish

1.75 litres/3 pints/7 1/2 cups vegetable stock

1 bunch fresh coriander (cilantro), roughly chopped

150ml/1/4 pint/2/3 cup single (light) cream, plus a little extra to garnish salt and ground black pepper

Instructions

Heat the oil in a large pan and fry the onions, stirring, for 5 minutes until soft. Add the potatoes, most of the beans (reserving a few for the garnish) and the stock, and bring to the boil. Simmer for 5 minutes, then add the coriander and simmer for a further 10 minutes.

Blend the soup in batches in a food processor or blender, then return to the rinsed pan.

Stir in the cream, season to taste, and bring to a simmer. Serve garnished with beans, cream and coriander sprigs.

Nutritional information per portion: Energy 358kcal/1504kJ; Protein 14.3g; Carbohydrate 46.4g, of which sugars 10.1g; Fat 14.2g, of which saturates 5.6g; Cholesterol 21mg; Calcium 156mg; Fibre 10.9g; Sodium 44mg.

Barbecued mini ribs

SERVES 6–8

1 sheet of pork ribs, about 675g/1 1/2lb

90ml/6 tbsp sweet oloroso sherry

15ml/1 tbsp tomato purée (paste)

5ml/1 tsp soy sauce

2.5ml/1/2 tsp Tabasco sauce

15ml/1 tbsp light muscovado (brown) sugar

30ml/2 tbsp seasoned plain (all-purpose) flour coarse sea salt

Instructions

Separate the ribs, then, using a meat cleaver or heavy knife, cut each rib in half widthways to make about 30 pieces.

Mix the sherry, tomato purée, soy sauce, Tabasco and sugar together in a bowl.

Stir in 2.5ml/1/2 tsp salt.

Put the seasoned flour in a strong plastic bag, then add the ribs and toss to coat. Dip each rib in the sauce. Cook on a hot barbecue or under a hot grill (broiler) for 30–40 minutes, turning occasionally until cooked and a little charred. Sprinkle with salt and serve.

COOK'S TIP

Oloroso sherry has a full body and sweet flavour sometimes reminiscent of port.

Nutritional information per portion: Energy 469kcal/1977kJ; Protein 15g; Carbohydrate 66.7g, of which sugars 3.9g; Fat 16.8g, of which saturates 5.5g; Cholesterol 38mg; Calcium 193mg; Fibre 2.7g; Sodium 1146mg.

Vegetable rice pot

SERVES 4

1 large aubergine (eggplant)

45ml/3 tbsp olive oil

2 onions, quartered and sliced

2 garlic cloves, finely chopped

1 red (bell) pepper, halved, seeded and sliced

1 yellow (bell) pepper, halved, seeded and sliced

200g/7oz fine green beans, halved

115g/4oz/1 1/2 cups brown cap (cremini) mushrooms, halved

300g/11oz/1 1/2 cups paella rice, washed and drained

1 dried chilli, seeded and crumbled

1 litre/1 3/4 pints/4 cups chicken stock

115g/4oz/1 cup peas

60ml/4 tbsp chopped fresh parsley

salt and ground black pepper

fresh parsley or coriander (cilantro) leaves, to garnish

Instructions

Halve the aubergine lengthways, then cut it into slices. Spread slices out in a large colander or on a draining board, sprinkle with salt and leave for about 30 minutes. Rinse under cold running water and pat dry with kitchen paper.

Heat 30ml/2 tbsp olive oil in a deep, wide frying pan or sauté pan over a high heat. Add the aubergine slices and sauté until golden, stirring occasionally, then transfer to kitchen paper to drain.

Add the remaining oil to the pan and cook the onion, and garlic until soft. Add the peppers, green beans and mushrooms and cook briefly. Add the drained rice and stir for 1–2 minutes, then stir in the aubergine. Add the chilli and seasoning. Add the stock. Add the peas and parsley and mix together.

Bring the mixture up to boiling point, then cover and cook over a low heat, for 20–25 minutes, checking the liquid level towards the end (the rice should absorb the liquid, but not burn). When the rice is tender, turn off the heat, cover the pan and leave to stand for 10 minutes for the remaining liquid to be absorbed. Garnish with the parsley or coriander and serve immediately.

Nutritional information per portion: Energy 454kcal/1891kJ; Protein 11.8g; Carbohydrate 78.3g, of which sugars 13.2g; Fat 10.4g, of which saturates 1.5g; Cholesterol 0mg; Calcium 98mg; Fibre 7.4g; Sodium 13mg.

Butterflied prawns in chocolate sauce

SERVES 4

8 large raw prawns (shrimp), in the shell

15ml/1 tbsp seasoned plain (all-purpose) flour

15ml/1 tbsp pale dry sherry juice of 1 large orange

15g/1/2oz dark (bittersweet) chocolate, chopped

30ml/2 tbsp olive oil

2 garlic cloves, finely chopped

2.5cm/1in piece fresh root ginger, finely chopped

1 small dried chilli, seeded and chopped salt and ground black pepper

Instructions

Peel the prawns, leaving just the tail sections intact. Make a shallow cut down the back of each one and pull out and discard the dark tract.

Turn the prawns over so that the undersides are uppermost, and then cut them open from tail to top, almost to the central back line.

Press the prawns down firmly to flatten them. Coat with the flour and set aside. Gently heat the sherry and orange juice in a pan. When warm, remove from the heat and stir in the chopped chocolate until melted.

Heat the oil in a large frying pan. Add the chopped garlic, ginger and chilli and cook for 2 minutes until golden. Remove with a slotted spoon and reserve. Add the prawns, cut side down, and cook for 2–3 minutes until golden brown with pink edges. Turn them and cook for a further 2 minutes.

Return the garlic mixture to the pan and add the chocolate sauce. Cook for 1 minute, turning the prawns to coat them in the sauce. Season and serve hot.

Nutritional information per portion: Energy 125kcal/520kJ; Protein 8.5g; Carbohydrate 6.5g, of which sugars 3.6g; Fat 6.9g, of which saturates 1.5g; Cholesterol 88mg; Calcium 44mg; Fibre 0.2g; Sodium 88mg.

Stuffed tomatoes and peppers

SERVES 4

2 large tomatoes

1 green (bell) pepper

1 yellow or orange (bell) pepper

75ml/5 tbsp olive oil

2 onions, finely chopped

2 garlic cloves, finely chopped

75g/3oz/3/4 cup almonds, chopped

175g/6oz/11/2 cups cooked rice, or 75g/3oz/scant

1/2 cup long grain rice, cooked and drained

30ml/2 tbsp Malaga raisins or muscatels, soaked in hot water

30ml/2 tbsp chopped fresh mint

45ml/3 tbsp chopped fresh flat leaf parsley, plus extra to garnish salt and ground black pepper

Instructions

Preheat the oven to 190°C/375°F/Gas 5. Cut the tomatoes in half and scoop out the pulp and seeds.

Put the tomato halves on kitchen paper with the cut sides down and leave to drain. Roughly chop the centres and seeds and place in a bowl.

Halve the peppers, leaving the cores intact. Scoop out the seeds. Brush the peppers with 15ml/1 tbsp of the oil.

Fry the onions and garlic in 30ml/2 tbsp oil. Stir in most of the almonds. Add the rice, tomato pulp, drained raisins, mint and 30ml/2 tbsp parsley. Season well, then spoon the mixture into the vegetable cases.

Bake uncovered for 20 minutes. Finely chop the remaining almonds and parsley in a food processor and sprinkle over the top. Drizzle with 15–30ml/1–2 tbsp olive oil. Return to the oven and bake for a further 20 minutes, or until turning golden. Serve, garnished with more chopped parsley.

Nutritional information per portion: Energy 365kcal/1522kJ; Protein 7.1g; Carbohydrate 28.6g, of which sugars 13.7g; Fat 25.5g, of which saturates 3.1g; Cholesterol 0mg; Calcium 95mg; Fibre 3.7g; Sodium 20mg.

Sherried onion soup with saffron

SERVES 4

40g/1 1/2oz/3 tbsp butter

2 large yellow onions, thinly sliced

1 small garlic clove, finely chopped

pinch of saffron threads (0.25g)

50g/2oz blanched almonds, toasted and finely ground

750ml/1 1/4 pints/3 cups chicken or vegetable stock

45ml/3 tbsp fino sherry

2.5ml/1/2 tsp paprika

salt and ground black pepper

FOR THE GARNISH

30ml/2 tbsp flaked or sliced almonds, toasted chopped fresh parsley

Instructions

Melt the butter in a heavy pan over a low heat. Add the onions and garlic, stirring to ensure that they are thoroughly coated in the melted butter, then cover the pan and cook very gently, stirring frequently, for about 20 minutes, or until the onions are soft and golden yellow.

Add the saffron threads to the pan and cook, uncovered, for 3–4 minutes, then add the finely ground almonds and cook, stirring the ingredients constantly, for a further 2–3 minutes. Pour the chicken or vegetable stock and sherry into the pan and stir in 5ml/1 tsp salt and the paprika. Season with plenty of black pepper. Bring to the boil, then lower the heat and simmer gently for about 10 minutes.

Pour the soup into a food processor and process until smooth, then return it to the rinsed pan. Reheat slowly, without allowing the soup to boil, stirring occasionally. Taste for seasoning, adding more salt and pepper if required. Ladle the soup into heated bowls, garnish with the toasted flaked or sliced almonds and a little chopped fresh parsley and serve immediately.

Nutritional information per portion: Energy 246kcal/1017kJ; Protein 5.5g; Carbohydrate 9.5g, of which sugars 6.7g; Fat 19.6g, of which saturates 6.1g; Cholesterol 21mg; Calcium 76mg; Fibre 2.9g; Sodium 68mg.

Menestra

SERVES 6

15ml/1 tbsp olive oil

115g/4oz streaky (fatty) bacon lardons or diced pancetta

1 onion, chopped

3 garlic cloves, finely chopped

90ml/6 tbsp chopped fresh parsley

175ml/6fl oz/3/4 cup dry white wine

150g/5oz green beans

200g/7oz bunched young carrots

6 small new potatoes, scrubbed

300ml/10fl oz/11/4 cups chicken stock

1 corn cob, kernels removed (optional)

200g/7oz/2 cups peas

50g/2oz mangetouts (snow peas)

salt and ground black pepper

2 hard-boiled eggs, chopped, to garnish

Instructions

Heat the oil in a large, heavy pan and fry the bacon or pancetta over a gentle heat for about 5 minutes, or until it crisps. Remove with a slotted spoon and reserve. Add the onion to the pan and cook in the bacon fat until softened, adding the garlic towards the end.

Remove the cooked onion to a food processor, add 30ml/2 tbsp of the chopped parsley and purée with a little of the white wine.

Prepare the vegetables. Cut the beans into short lengths, and the carrots to the same size. Bring a pan of salted water to the boil and add the potatoes. Cook for about 10 minutes. Add the carrots to the pan of potatoes, and cook for a further 5 minutes.

Meanwhile, return the bacon to the other pan and add the stock. Put in the beans, corn kernels and peas and lay the mangetouts over the top. Half cover the pan and leave to simmer for 5–10 minutes, until the vegetables are just cooked. Drain the potatoes and carrots and add them to the pan.

Add the rest of the wine and the onion purée to the pan, warming the liquid and turning the vegetables gently with a wooden spoon. Check the seasoning, adding more if necessary, and serve with the juices. Garnish with chopped egg and the remaining parsley.

Nutritional information per portion: Energy 207kcal/865kJ; Protein 8.1g; Carbohydrate 23.4g, of which sugars 9.6g; Fat 7.6g, of which saturates 2.1g; Cholesterol 12mg; Calcium 68mg; Fibre 5.5g; Sodium 274mg.

Lentils with mushrooms and anis

SERVES 4

30ml/2 tbsp olive oil

1 large onion, sliced

2 garlic cloves, finely chopped

250g/9oz/3 cups brown cap (cremini) mushrooms, sliced

150g/5oz/generous 1/2 cup brown or green lentils

4 tomatoes, cut in eighths

1 bay leaf

25g/1oz/1/2 cup chopped fresh parsley

30ml/2 tbsp anis spirit or anisette

salt, paprika and black pepper

Instructions

Heat the oil in a large, heavy pan. Add the sliced onion and fry gently over a low heat, with the garlic, until softened but not browned.

Add the sliced mushrooms and stir to combine with the onion and garlic.

Continue cooking, stirring gently, for a couple of minutes.

Add the lentils, tomato wedges and bay leaf with 175ml/6fl oz/3/4 cup water. Simmer gently, covered, for 30–40 minutes until the lentils are soft, and the liquid has almost disappeared.

Stir in the chopped parsley and anis. Season with salt, paprika and black pepper.

Nutritional information per portion: Energy 242kcal/1018kJ; Protein 12.5g; Carbohydrate 29.8g, of which sugars 9.5g; Fat 7.2g, of which saturates 1g; Cholesterol 0mg; Calcium 83mg; Fibre 6.9g; Sodium 23mg.

Chicken croquettes

SERVES 4

25g/1oz/2 tbsp butter

25g/1oz/1/4 cup plain (all-purpose) flour

150ml/1/4 pint/2/3 cup milk

15ml/1 tbsp olive oil, plus extra for deep-frying 1 boneless chicken breast with skin, diced

1 garlic clove, finely chopped

1 small egg, beaten

50g/2oz/1 cup stale white breadcrumbs salt and ground black pepper fresh flat leaf parsley, to garnish

lemon wedges, to serve

Instructions

Melt the butter in a pan. Add the flour and cook gently, stirring, for 1 minute.

Gradually stir in the milk and cook until smooth and thick. Cover and set aside.

Heat the oil in a frying pan and fry the diced chicken and garlic together, turning, for 5 minutes.

When the chicken is lightly browned and cooked through, put the contents of the frying pan into a food processor and process until finely chopped. Add the mixture to the sauce and stir to combine. Season to taste, then leave to cool.

Once cooled and firm, shape the mixture into eight small sausage shapes. Dip each one in beaten egg, then roll in breadcrumbs to coat.

Heat the oil in a pan, until a cube of bread dropped in the oil browns in 1 minute. Lower the croquettes into the oil and cook for 4 minutes until crisp and golden, then drain on kitchen paper. Serve with lemon wedges and garnish with parsley.

Nutritional information per portion: Energy 286kcal/1195kJ; Protein 13.9g; Carbohydrate 16.4g, of which sugars 2.2g; Fat 18.9g, of which saturates 5.8g; Cholesterol 89mg; Calcium 80mg; Fibre 0.5g; Sodium 189mg.

Amanida

SERVES 6

1 lolla green lettuce

50g/2oz cured, sliced chorizo or in a piece skinned and diced

4 thin slices Serrano ham

130g/4½oz can sardines in oil, drained

130g/4½oz can tuna steak in oil, drained

8 canned white asparagus spears, drained

2–3 canned palm hearts, drained 115g/4oz/⅔ cup tiny arbequina olives

115g/4oz/⅔ cup big gordas or queen olives, preferably purplish ones 10 medium tomatoes

15ml/1 tbsp chopped fresh parsley, to garnish

FOR THE VINAIGRETTE

1 garlic clove, split lengthways

30ml/2 tbsp sherry vinegar

30ml/2 tbsp red wine vinegar

60ml/4 tbsp olive oil

60ml/4 tbsp extra virgin olive oil

salt and ground black pepper

Instructions

Make the vinaigrette. Wipe the cut side of the garlic round a large bowl, then discard. Whisk the other ingredients together in the bowl.

Break the stem ends off eight lettuce leaves, dip the leaves into the vinaigrette and arrange them around a large serving plate.

Position the chorizo slices or dice on one side of the plate. Roll the ham and arrange opposite. Drain and blot the fish, then arrange across the plate in a cross. Put the asparagus, spears outwards, and the palm hearts (split lengthways), on opposite sides of the plate. Pile the olives in the spaces.

Put the tomatoes in a bowl and pour over boiling water. Leave to stand for 10 minutes, then drain. Peel and quarter six of the tomatoes and cut out the centres. Arrange the tomatoes, round side up, in the centre of the plate to make a flower shape. Brush vinaigrette dressing over the tomatoes, palm hearts and asparagus and season lightly. Sprinkle the parsley on the tomatoes and white vegetables. Serve at room temperature.

Nutritional information per portion: Energy 638kcal/2671kJ; Protein 74.6g; Carbohydrate 9.8g, of which sugars 9.8g; Fat 33.7g, of which saturates 7.3g; Cholesterol 218mg; Calcium 183mg; Fibre 3.1g; Sodium 4618mg.

Moors and Christians

SERVES 6

400g/14oz/2 cups black beans, soaked overnight

1 onion

1 carrot

1 celery stick

1 garlic clove, finely chopped

1 bay leaf

1.75l/3 pints/2 cups water

5ml/1 tsp paprika

45ml/3 tbsp olive oil

juice of 1 orange

300g/11oz/1 1/2 cups long grain rice

salt and cayenne pepper

FOR THE GARNISH

chopped fresh parsley

thin wedges of orange

sliced red onion

Instructions

Put the beans in a pan with the onion, carrot, celery, garlic, bay leaf and water. Bring to the boil and cook rapidly for 10 minutes, then reduce the heat and simmer for 1 hour. Top up the water, if necessary. When the beans are almost tender, drain, discarding the vegetables and bay leaf. Return the beans to a clean pan.

Blend the paprika and oil with cayenne pepper to taste and stir into the beans with the orange juice. Top up with water, if necessary. Heat until barely simmering, then cover and cook for 15 minutes until the beans are tender. Remove from the heat and allow to stand for 15 minutes. Season with salt.

Cook the rice until tender. Drain, then pack into moulds and leave for 10 minutes. Transfer the rice to serving plates and arrange the beans around the edges. Garnish with the parsley, orange and red onion.

Nutritional information per portion: Energy 445kcal/1875kJ; Protein 19.7g; Carbohydrate 77.8g, of which sugars 3.2g; Fat 7g, of which saturates 1.1g; Cholesterol 0mg; Calcium 68mg; Fibre 5.6g; Sodium 12mg.

Manufactured by Amazon.ca
Bolton, ON